Gender Dimensions of Investment Climate Reform

Gender Dimensions of Investment Climate Reform

A Guide for Policy Makers
and Practitioners

THE WORLD BANK
Washington, D.C.

© 2010 The International Bank for Reconstruction and Development / The World Bank
1818 H Street NW
Washington DC 20433
Telephone: 202-473-1000
Internet: www.worldbank.org
E-mail: feedback@worldbank.org

1 2 3 4 12 11 10 09

This volume is a product of the staff of the International Bank for Reconstruction and Development / The World Bank. The findings, interpretations, and conclusions expressed in this volume do not necessarily reflect the views of the Executive Directors of The World Bank or the governments they represent.

The World Bank does not guarantee the accuracy of the data included in this work. The boundaries, colors, denominations, and other information shown on any map in this work do not imply any judgement on the part of The World Bank concerning the legal status of any territory or the endorsement or acceptance of such boundaries.

Rights and Permissions

ISBN: 978-0-8213-8095-6
eISBN: 978-0-8213-8098-7
DOI: 10.1596/978-0-8213-8095-6

Cover: Naylor Design, Inc.

Library of Congress Cataloging-in-Publication Data

Simavi, Sevi.
Gender dimensions of investment climate reform : a guide for policy makers and practitioners / [by Sevi Simavi, Clare Manuel and Mark Blackden].
    p. cm.
 Includes bibliographical references and index.
 ISBN 978-0-8213-8095-6 — ISBN 978-0-8213-8098-7 (electronic)
1. Investments, Foreign—Moral and ethical aspects—Developing countries. 2. Women-owned business enterprises—Developing countries. 3. Sex discrimination against women—Developing countries. 4. Sex discrimination in employment—Developing countries. I. Manuel, Clare, 1962- II. Blackden, C. Mark, 1954- III. Title.
 HG5993.S56 2009
 332.67'3082091724—dc22

                                                                    2009032587

Contents

Contents

Boxes

Figures

Tables

Contents

Foreword

In the countries in which we work, whether we think of a small farm, a small-scale manufacturer, or a small services company, the owner most likely is a woman. Expanding women's economic opportunities is smart business and increasingly seen as one of the most important driving forces behind economic growth and the fight against poverty.

Since IFC instituted its Gender Program in 2004, we have been able to demonstrate that investing in women entrepreneurs makes sense from both a development and a business perspective. We have been able to catalyze investments to women entrepreneurs through commercial banks, helping them understand the business opportunities in banking women. We have been able to provide support to organizations working with women entrepreneurs to increase the quality of their business planning and development.

Now, at this time of global economic crisis, IFC is focused on the legal, regulatory, and institutional reforms necessary to foster women's entrepreneurship, building on our extensive experience working with governments on business-enabling environment reforms. This spirit of crisis provides an unprecedented opportunity to take action on transforming regulations, economies, and people's lives. Countries that do not capitalize on 50 percent of their human resources run the risk of severely undermining their competitiveness and hindering their economic growth. Capturing this "missed potential" offers tremendous opportunities for development.

What types of policies and strategies are needed to capture the potential of women to drive economic growth? How can policy makers effectively tackle the challenges faced by women entrepreneurs? With *Gender Dimensions of Investment Climate Reform: A Guide for Policy Makers and Practitioners*, we want to offer solutions and encourage change by providing policy makers with tools they need to focus on the potential of women entrepreneurs. This book provides thought leadership on common policy and regulatory issues that face women entrepreneurs and analyzes key investment climate areas with a gender lens. The book also presents practical and replicable tools for designing policies that will empower women in business and unlock countries' full economic potential.

We trust that integrating gender issues into the investment climate agenda will catalyze support to the productive role women play in private sector development. Failing to unleash the economic growth potential of women business owners has always been shortsighted. At a time of global economic uncertainty, it is a luxury few nations can afford. IFC hopes this guide will provide a path forward to a place where smart business underpins smart growth.

Rachel Kyte
Vice President, Business Advisory Services
IFC

Acknowledgments

This book has been coauthored by Sevi Simavi, Clare Manuel, and Mark Blackden. The authors gratefully acknowledge Brenda Brainch, Richard Hooper, Fiona MacCulloch, Deborah Mansfield (all of The Law & Development Partnership); Caroline Pinder (WISE Development); Professor Patrick McAuslan (Birkbeck College, University of London); and Professor Stephanie Seguino (University of Vermont) for their intellectual contributions to individual modules and for providing advice and guidance. The authors are most grateful for the guidance, oversight, and support received from Zouera Youssoufou, Monika Weber-Fahr, Pierre Guislain, Cecilia Sager, and Cecile Fruman throughout the entire process.

Thoughtful comments and suggestions enhanced the overall quality of this publication. Individual chapters were refereed by a panel of IFC experts comprising Natalie Africa, Gokhan Akinci, Alejandro Alvarez de la Campa, Gina Barbieri, Sonali Bishop, Lada Busevac, Alberto Crisculo, Natalia Cubillos, Julien Galant, Tania Ghossein, Armando Heilborn, Eduardo Hernandez, Benjamin Herzberg, Dobromir Hristov, Ankur Huria, Alan David Johnson, Dushan Kovacevic, Bartol Leticia, Jan Loeprick, Sumit Manchanda, Andrei Mihknev, Shokraneh Minovi, Komal Mohindra, Carmen Niethammer, Celia Ortega, Daniela Perovic, Anja Robakowski-Van Stralen, Frank Sader, Markus Scheuermaier, Uma Subramanian, Denis Torkhov, Stefan Van Parys, Robert Whyte, and Everett Wohlers.

Fieldwork to prepare Gender and Investment Climate Reform Assessments (GICRAs) in five Pacific countries—Samoa, Solomon Islands, Timor-Leste, Tonga, and Vanuatu—in February and March 2009 provided an opportunity to test an earlier draft of the guide. The authors are grateful for the leadership and interest of Sonali Bishop, team leader for the GICRA reports, and for the valuable contributions and insights from the teams of local lawyers and economists who undertook the GICRA work in each of the countries, as well as from participants in country-level businesswomen's forums.

The full draft was also reviewed by a World Bank Group expert panel comprising Nadereh Chamlou, Amanda Ellis, Teresa Genta-Fons, Mary Hallward-Driemeier, Andrew Morrison, Vincent Palmade, Rita Ramalho, Mehnaz Safavian, and Sarosh Sattar.

In addition, the authors gratefully acknowledge the invaluable comments received from donor partners, including Christine Brendel (GTZ); Jannine Cocker (CIDA); Lisa Tessa Fairman, Loga Gnanasambanthan, Harry Hagan, Paul Healey, Xavier Lecacheur, and Richard Sandall (all DFID); Jessica Ebbeler (Millennium Challenge Corporation); Stefani Klos (KfW); Albena Melin (SIDA); and Hege Bakke Sorreime (NORAD).

We are most appreciative of the help we received from Stephen McGroarty, Rick Ludwick, and Nora Ridolfi at the World Bank Office of the Publisher and Arlette Baliki, Anna Hidalgo, and Rafael Pinto, who supported us throughout the production process.

Finally, we are deeply indebted to the governments of the United Kingdom and Canada for funding this project. Without their generous support, this publication would not have been possible.

About the Authors

Sevi Simavi is a lawyer with expertise in the areas of private and financial sector development. She currently spearheads IFC's work on gender and investment climate; designs global projects; develops new approaches; and promotes laws, policies, and institutions that foster women entrepreneurs and increase their participation in the private sector. During her tenure at the World Bank Group, she initiated, developed, and rolled out IFC's secured lending advisory product and led or contributed to over 30 research and operational projects on business regulation, commercial, and insolvency law reform around the globe. Prior to joining the World Bank Group, Sevi practiced international business law. She holds law degrees from Georgetown University Law Center, Washington, DC, and Marmara University School of Law, Istanbul.

Clare Manuel is a UK lawyer with particular expertise in the areas of investment climate reform and private sector development in developing countries. She works with governments to develop accessible commercial law and policy frameworks that are relevant to both foreign and local investors. Having gained her initial experience in a City of London commercial law firm, she has acquired more than 20 years' experience in working at senior levels in government—in the United Kingdom, Africa, the Caribbean, and the South Pacific. As a founder and director of the Law & Development Partnership, she has advised extensively on private sector development, justice, and gender issues in developing countries.

Mark Blackden is an independent consultant to the World Bank Group, United Nations Development Programme (UNDP), and other international institutions. Earlier, he worked for more than 25 years in the World Bank, where he had wide-ranging operational experience in Sub-Saharan Africa, focusing on public sector management and technical assistance programs, participatory development, design and delivery of training, and gender and development. He managed the Region's gender program over the period of 1996–2007. Mark obtained an MSc in International Relations from Georgetown University and a BA in German and French from the University of Kent at Canterbury.

Abbreviations

ADR	Alternative Dispute Resolution
CEDAW	UN Convention on Elimination of All Forms of Discrimination Against Women
CCT	Compliance Cost Tool
CIDA	The Canadian International Development Agency
DHS	Demographic and health survey
DFID	Department for International Development (UK)
DP	Development partner
EPZ	Export Processing Zone
FAO	Food and Agriculture Organization
FDI	Foreign direct investment
FGD	Focus group discussion
FHH	Female-headed household
FIAS	Foreign Investment Advisory Service (World Bank/International Finance Corporation)
FinScope	Specialized Household Survey of Financial Services Usage (South Africa)
GGA	Gender and Growth Assessment
GTZ	German Technical Cooperation Agency
HIV/AIDS	Human Immunodeficiency Virus/Acquired Immunodeficiency Syndrome
IC	Investment climate
IFC	International Finance Corporation
ILO	International Labour Organization
IPP	Investment policy and promotion
MDGs	Millennium Development Goals
MHH	Male-headed household
NGO	Nongovernmental organization
PPD	Public-private dialogue

SCM	Standard Cost Model
SEZ	Special Economic Zone
SME	Small and Medium Enterprise
UN	United Nations
UNDP	United Nations Development Program
UNIDO	United Nations Industrial Development Organization
UNIFEM	United Nations Development Fund for Women
VAT	Value-added tax

Introduction and Economic Rationale

Purpose and Structure of the Guide

Promoting women's economic empowerment is increasingly seen as an important driving force behind economic growth and the fight against poverty. Women's economic participation as entrepreneurs, employees, and leaders is recognized as a measure of a country's economic viability and dynamism.

Although women's entrepreneurship is on the rise globally and female labor force participation has increased substantially in recent years, significant disparities still exist. In the developing world, women are more likely to work in the informal economy, where they are subject to inefficiencies and limitations more often than men. In many regions women are less likely to have land and often are disadvantaged by prevailing laws and regulations that prevent them from being able to hold title. In addition to problems faced by all entrepreneurs, women frequently face gender bias in the socioeconomic environment when it comes to establishing and developing their own enterprises and accessing economic resources. These not only disadvantage women but also reduce the growth potential, productivity, and performance of the economy as a whole. Gender-based inequalities impose significant development costs on societies.

This guide aims to provide fresh thinking to solve common issues women entrepreneurs face in the investment climate area. It presents actionable, practical, replicable, and scalable tools. Specifically, the guide seeks to enable development practitioners and policy makers who are not gender specialists to (i) diagnose gender issues in an investment climate reform area, (ii) design practical solutions and recommendations to address gender constraints, and (iii) include effective monitoring and evaluation tools to oversee the implementation of those recommendations.

While the guide is primarily directed to project leaders in IFC and World Bank Group managing investment climate reform projects, it will also be of use to a wider audience, including policy makers, the donor community, women's business associations, academics, think tanks, and development practitioners who have an interest in gender and private sector development issues. As this is an innovative area of work, feedback on new initiatives, policies, and research is welcomed and will be incorporated into the guide's later versions.

The analysis, conclusions, and recommendations presented in this guide are based on gender and economic theory, analysis of country case studies and practices, the IFC's own experience, reform experience in a number of emerging market countries, and interviews with development practitioners, policy makers, and academics. It should be noted that gender equality is a complex and multifaceted topic with several dimensions. The guide tackles gender issues only through a private sector development lens, aims to promote gender-sensitive investment climate reforms that would equally benefit women as well as men and offers some practical policy solutions.

The guide starts with a brief section on the *economic rationale* for gender inclusion in investment climate reform work. It is then divided into nine modules. Recognizing the socioeconomic dimensions of gender-focused work, the *core module* outlines the broader, overarching framework within which gender-informed investment climate work can take place. It also focuses on the monitoring and evaluation framework, with particular emphasis on establishing appropriate baselines to facilitate the measurement of gender-informed changes in the business environment. The *eight thematic modules* provide specific guidance on key investment climate issues comprising (i) public-private dialogue, (ii) business start-up and operation, (iii) business taxation, (iv) trade logistics, (v) secured lending, (vi) alternative dispute resolution, (vii) special economic zones, and (viii) foreign investment policy and promotion. Thematic modules are designed to guide the reader through the project cycle and present the three-step process: (i) diagnostic, (ii) solution design, and (iii) implementation and monitoring and evaluation. Although each module is designed to be used on a standalone basis, each should be read with reference to the core module. There is therefore some repetition across modules and cross-referencing between them.

Why Gender Matters in Investment Climate Reform

An awareness of gender issues is important when considering strategies to improve the business environment and promote private sector development. Creating greater economic opportunities for women has compelling economic reasons, and inequalities impose development costs on societies.[1]

1 Unequal Distribution of Women's Economic Activities

Women are active economic participants as business owners, workers, and managers globally (table I.1, figure I.1). Women's entrepreneurship, which has been recognized as an important untapped source of economic growth, is on the rise globally,[2] and women's share of the labor force has also increased in recent years, reaching 40 percent worldwide by 2006.[3]

Despite these positive trends, women's economic activities are not equally distributed across the productive sectors. In most developing countries female-run enterprises tend to be undercapitalized, having poorer access to machinery, fertilizer, extension information, and credit than male-run enterprises. Laws, regulations, and customs restrict women's ability to manage property, conduct business, or even travel without their husbands' consent. Disparities also exist in women's workforce participation. Women are three times as likely as men to be hired informally[4] and are much more likely to be unpaid workers that contribute to the family's business than are men (figure I.2). Such discrepancies impair women's ability to participate in development and to contribute to higher living standards.

Table I.1: Enterprise Survey Data, Regional Summaries

	Percentage of full-time female workers	Percentage of women in senior management positions
All countries	27.43	9.13
Latin America & Caribbean	31.71	12.64
Eastern Europe & Central Asia	41.06	11.57
Sub-Saharan Africa	20.67	8.27
Middle East & North Africa	17.75	4.58
South Asia	18.78	1.56

Source: World Bank Enterprise Surveys.

Figure I.1   Female-Owned Firms across Regions

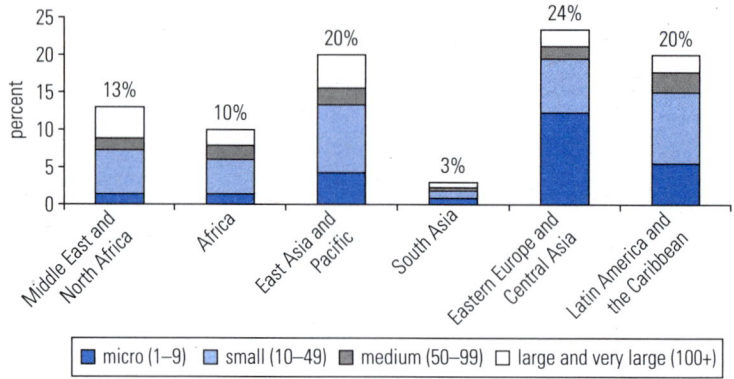

Source: World Bank Enterprise Surveys.

Figure I.2   Employment Status by Gender, 2007 (Ratio of Percentage of Females to Males)

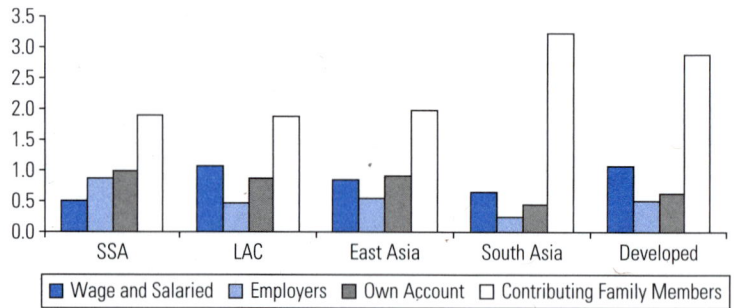

Source: ILO, *Global Employment Trends for Women 2008*.

2   What Gender Disparity Means for Policy Makers

Several aspects of gender relations—gender biases in rights; gender differences in access to and control over material resources, such as land, credit, employment and wages, as well as the gender-based division of labor; and disparities between males and females in power and decision making—have implications for well-being at the household level and, as a consequence, long-term productivity growth.

Today, in no country in the world do we observe absolute equality between men and women (figure I.3).[5] But closing the gender gap affects growth in several ways. Significant benefits have been found at the household level, with improvement in children's well-being. In particular, greater gender equality in education and income can enhance a woman's bargaining power within the household. Because women, more than men, tend to allocate spending to children's needs, education levels will increase, mortality rates will fall, and nutrition will improve. Greater gender equality, by therefore reducing undernourishment in children, will result in decreases in chronic sickness, stunting, and impaired social and cognitive development. The long-run macroeconomic effect, apart from improving individual well-being, is an improvement in human capital and thus the labor productivity of a society.[6]

In addition to the intergenerational benefits of gender equality, closing gender gaps in education and employment brings efficiency gains. From a competitiveness perspective, women's disproportionately low participation in the workforce and exclusion from employment—or employment discrimination that leads to occupational segregation—can reduce the pool of applicants, distort the allocation

Figure I.3   Global Gender Gap Index

Rank 2008	Country	Score*
1	Norway	0.824
2	Finland	0.820
3	Sweden	0.814
4	Iceland	0.800
5	New Zealand	0.786
126	Benin	0.558
127	Pakistan	0.554
128	Saudi Arabia	0.553
129	Chad	0.529
130	Yemen	0.466

*0 to 1 scale: 0 = inequality, 1 = equality

Source: World Economic Forum Global Gender Gap Index 2008.

of talent and the productivity of human capital, thereby reduce the average productivity of the labor force. Reducing inequalities in education and job access can stimulate economywide growth.[7] Moreover, gender gaps in education appear to have a negative effect on foreign direct investment.[8]

There also appear to be positive correlations between women's representation on corporate boards and corporate performance, suggesting that women are good for business. Fortune 500 firms with the highest percentage of women corporate officers yielded on average 35.1 percent greater return on equity and 34 percent greater total return to shareholders than those with the lowest percentages of women corporate officers.[9]

> Examining the comparative growth record of Indian states between 1961 and 1991 reveals that a 10 percent increase in the female-male ratio of workers would increase output by 8 percent, and a 10 percent increase in the female-male ratio of managers would increase output by 2 percent.[10]

In short, countries that do not fully capitalize on one-half of their human resources run the risk of undermining their competitive potential. Capturing this "missed potential" should be the goal of gender-informed investment climate reform, as the payoffs could be considerable.[11] Therefore, integrating gender dimensions into policy dialogue can reduce gender barriers, unleash the untapped productive potential of women, and broaden both the economic impact and sustainability of policy interventions.

3 Gender-Specific Challenges and Responses in Investment Climate Work

There are three fundamental and interrelated gender-specific challenges within investment climate work. First, women and men may have unequal legal status and property rights, with profound implications for women's economic capacity. Second, even when the laws and procedures are gender neutral in theory, they may still result in gender-biased outcomes that can have significant effects on access to and control of economic resources, which affect growth, productivity, and welfare. Finally, women are not well represented and have less access to networks and lobbies to influence public decision making (figure I.4). Investment climate programs can help reduce these biases through gender-specific policy responses.

3.1 Women's Unequal Legal Status

The legal and regulatory framework of a country, which is a core element of a well-functioning business environment, may be markedly different for women. Laws directly affecting women's capacity to participate in the private sector may include male consent to start or operate a business. Additional laws outside the business sector, such as those concerning marriage, family relations, and inheritance, may have a determining influence on women's ability to participate in the private sector.

Figure I.4   Gender Challenges in Investment Climate Work

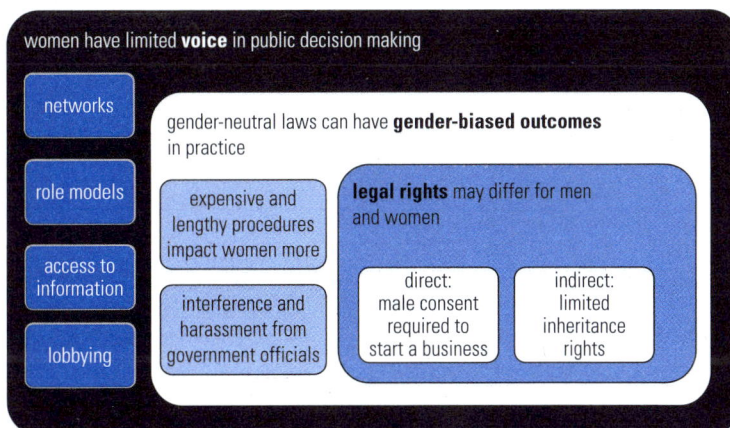

women have limited **voice** in public decision making

networks

role models

access to information

lobbying

gender-neutral laws can have **gender-biased outcomes** in practice

expensive and lengthy procedures impact women more

interference and harassment from government officials

legal rights may differ for men and women

direct: male consent required to start a business

indirect: limited inheritance rights

Source: Authors.

| Figure I.5 | Businesses in Uganda Responding That Government Officials Have "Interfered" in Their Business |

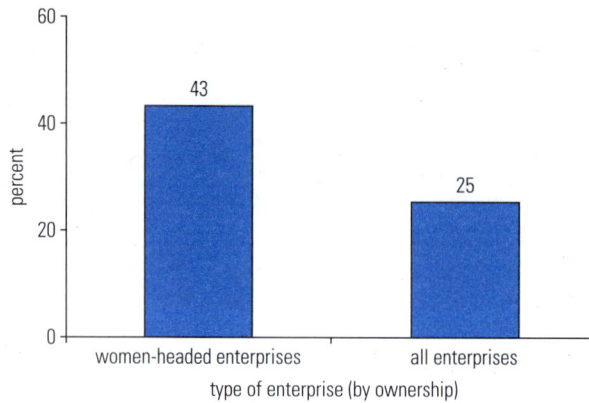

Source: Ellis et al 2006.

3.2   Gender-Neutral Laws but Gender-Biased Outcomes

Even a legal and regulatory environment that is "gender-neutral" in principle may have gender-differentiated outcomes. As a result, these laws may impede women to a greater extent than men when it comes to access to credit, assets, education, training, and information needed to start and operate a business.

Barriers to business formalization, particularly lengthy and complex registration, incorporation, and licensing practices, have a disproportionately negative effect on women, in some cases making it impossible for them to formalize. For example, women may be less able than men to afford long and expensive registration procedures, in part because of the "double workday" of domestic and business responsibilities or because they may face higher levels of "interference" in interacting with government officials or complying with government regulations (figure I.5). Moreover, women are often perceived as "softer targets" for corruption and are asked for "speed payments."

Similarly, the institutions involved in designing and implementing investment climate reforms may differ in terms of their accessibility to women and their understanding of how gender issues may affect their work, just as women may have less knowledge of reforms under way or planned and less access to relevant information.

A survey in **Bangladesh** found that government clerks who were charging "speed payments" to process claims were more likely to target women, as they were assumed to have a male provider. Pregnant and ill women were more likely to be subject to such "informal payments" because they were seen to be in a weak position to protest.

Source: UNIFEM 2008.

3.3 Women's Limited Voice and Power in Decision Making

Another commonly encountered constraint that can be addressed through investment climate work is that women, particularly in developing countries, have limited ability to influence decisions either in their community or at the national level. This may mean low representation in parliament, public office, and managerial positions in companies or corporate boards. Further, women are often excluded from informal networks of communication; and gender-based stereotypes and lack of role models often serve as barriers to women's professional advancement and limit their voices both in business communities and policy making. Including women business owners and women's business associations in public-private dialogue and advocacy efforts will allow women's unique constraints to be considered in the reform process.

The modules in this guide will discuss in detail how investment climate reform programs can practically and effectively address these challenges and ensure that women also equally benefit from reforms.

Notes

1. For an extensive treatment of the development costs of gender inequality, see A. Mason and Elizabeth M. King, "Engendering Development Through Gender Equality in Rights, Resources, and Voice," 35.

2. Richardson et al., "The Challenges of Growing Small Businesses: Insights from Women Entrepreneurs in Africa," iii.

3. World Bank, World Development Report, 2005.

4. World Bank, *How to Reform*, 18.

5. The data used for figure I.3 are from the World Economic Forum, which developed a composite measure of gender equality, the Gender Gap Index, which reflects differences in health, education, empowerment, and employment using 14 indicators with data from a wide variety of sources.

6. On intrahousehold resource allocation, see, for example, Blumberg. 1988. "Income Under Female Versus Male Control," *Journal of Family Issues*, 9 (1): 51–84 Haddad, Lawrence, John Hoddinott, and Harold Alderman. 1997. *Intrahousehold Resource Allocation in Developing Countries: Models, Methods, and Policy*. Baltimore, MD: Johns Hopkins University Press. 13.; Desai and Johnson. 2005. "Women's Decision-making and Child Health: Familial and Social Hierarchies." Paper commissioned by the Measure DHS project, in Calverton, Maryland. August.: 55–68.

7. See, for example, Stephen Knowles, Paula Lorgelly, and P. Dorian Owen, "Are Educational Gender Gaps a Brake on Economic Development? Some Cross-Country Empirical Evidence," *Oxford Economic Papers* 54 (1): 118–49; S. Klasen and F. Lamanna, "The Impact of Gender Inequality in Education and Employment on Economic Growth in Developing Countries," *Feminist Economics* 15 (3): 91–132; B. Esteve-Volart, "Gender Discrimination and Growth: Theory and Evidence from India," 1–68; A. Boschini, "The Impact of Gender Stereotypes on Economic Growth" (Department of Economics, University of Stockholm, 2003); T. Cavalcanti and J. Tavares, "The Output Cost of Gender Discrimination: A Model-Based Macroeconomic Estimate" (Universidade Nova de Lisboa and Center for Economic Policy Research, 2007).

8. Matthias Busse and Peter Nunnenkamp, "Gender disparity in education and international competition for foreign direct investment." *Feminist Economics* 15 (3): 61–90. Some skepticism remains about the reliability of results from cross-country growth regressions, in part due to concern about simultaneity problems (between gross domestic product growth and gender equality). Two studies that address this problem, using 3SLS estimation techniques, are Baliamoune-Lutz, "Globalisation and Gender Inequality: Is Africa Different?" *Journal of African Economies* 16 (2): 301–348; and Stephanie Seguino and James Lovinsky, "The Impact of Religiosity on Gender Attitudes and Outcomes" (UNRISD, 2009). Results from macroeconomic research on gender and

growth, surveyed in Janet G. Stotsky, *Gender and Its Relevance to Macroeconomic Policy: A Survey*, (International Monetary Fund, 2006) are consistent with the microeconomic research. Although causality is difficult to conclusively establish because of limited time series data, this combined body of work offers a convergence of evidence on the benefits of gender equality in education and, to a lesser extent, employment, for societal economic well-being.

9. Catalyst, "The Bottom Line: Connecting Corporate Performance and Gender Diversity," 2004.

10. T. Besley, R. Burgess, and B. Esteve-Volart, "Operationalising Pro-Poor Growth: India Case Study" (DFID, 2004).

11. This is, essentially, why the World Bank Group and its partners have embarked on a Gender Action Plan, at the core of which is "gender equality as smart economics." For more on the Gender Action Plan, see www.worldbank.org/gender. Awareness of gender in the development agenda has grown considerably and has been bolstered by mounting empirical evidence of the costs of gender inequality for development and by greater recognition of the centrality of addressing gender as integral to development effectiveness.

Gender-Informed Baseline for Diagnostics, Solution Design, Implementation, and Monitoring and Evaluation

The introductory chapter made the case for why gender issues need to be integrated into investment climate reform. This core module sets out the *baseline framework* for addressing the gender dimensions of investment climate reform through each of the key phases of diagnostics, solution design, and implementation and monitoring and evaluation. Before delving into any particular investment climate constraint, it is critical to establish a baseline of common elements needed to underpin a gender-informed understanding of the investment climate and to support design and implementation of appropriate solutions.

This core module should be used alongside each of the eight modules in this guide, as it provides a broader context as well as an essential foundation for each of the specific topics the modules tackle.

Summary

CORE MODULE

Step 1   Core Diagnostics

1.1   Understand the Roles of Men and Women in the Economy

1.1.1   *Analyze the Business Sector through a Gender Lens*

The starting point for an investment climate reform is an analysis of the economy—of key sectors and potential areas for growth, and of the structure and nature of the business community. Such an analysis should include a review of the roles and status of men and women in the economy—as entrepreneurs, employers, and workers.

Men and women often operate in different sectors of the economy and at different levels of economic activity. Patterns differ by region and by sector (table 1). In Sub-Saharan Africa women are more likely to work in agriculture than men, but the reverse is true in Latin America and the Caribbean. It is important to avoid stereotypes that assume that women are always concentrated in smaller businesses or in specific sectors (such as garments). Instead, a careful country-specific analysis is required to determine the extent to which men and women entrepreneurs are involved in manufacturing, industrial production, or in service-oriented activities, including trade.

The employment status of women and men can vary widely, too. In Latin America and the Caribbean, women are more heavily represented in wage work than in self-employment, but the opposite pattern exists in Sub-Saharan Africa. In all countries, though, women are less likely to be employers than men. Women are much more likely to be unpaid workers who contribute to a family business than are men (International Labour Organization [ILO] 2008).

Knowing where men and women are situated in the economy, and what their principal economic activities are, enables investment climate reform to be targeted more effectively to meet the different obstacles and constraints they face. Conversely, ignoring gender differences can render pro–private sector interventions less

Table 1: Female and Male Employment by Sector, 2007 (in percentages)

Region	Agriculture		Industry		Services	
	Women	Men	Women	Men	Women	Men
Sub-Saharan Africa	68	62	6	12	26	25
Latin America/Caribbean	11	25	15	27	75	48
East Asia	41	36	26	28	34	36
South Asia	61	43	18	23	21	34
Developed countries	3	5	13	34	84	61

Source: ILO, Global Employment Trends for Women 2008.

effective. Specifically, identifying key sectors in which women predominate or play an important economic role is important in analyzing sector-specific constraints to business registration, licensing, and taxation, so that, as needed, a more gender-responsive approach can be developed. This is especially important as a means of informing policies and strategies with respect to special economic zones (module 7) and to foreign investment policy and promotion (module 8). Linking an understanding of economic roles with analysis of gender differences in access to resources facilitates identification of important gaps and missed opportunities (box 1).

Data are available from World Bank Enterprise Surveys on many of the core characteristics of businesses, including sector of operation, size, location, years in operation, and management structure. In some instances, especially in the more recent surveys, the information can be disaggregated by the gender of the business owner, which provides a foundation for profiling where men and women are in the enterprise sector and where there are differences in key enterprise characteristics. Table 2 shows such data for a small sample of African countries.

1.1.2   *Take Account of Nonmarket Work and Time Use*

Because women face a disproportionate burden of domestic tasks, it is important to collect data, where available, on this division of labor. Especially in low-income countries and among the poor in all countries, women work more hours per day than men (box 2), as revealed in time-allocation data the world over.[1] The "double workday" of women places disproportionate pressure on them and limits their ability to engage in income-generating activities, own and operate businesses, and participate in community or national decision making.

To a considerable extent, therefore, women can only engage in directly productive economic activity after discharge of or concurrent with domestic responsibilities. Thus investment climate reforms aimed at simplifying procedures (notably reducing

---

BOX 1   **Gender Gaps and Missed Potential in Kenya**

Women in **Kenya** manage 40 percent of smallholder farms, but they receive only 1 percent of the total amount of credit directed to agriculture and receive lower levels of agricultural inputs, such as extension services, than their male counterparts. It has been estimated that increasing female access to such inputs to the same level as men's would increase agricultural yields in Kenya by more than 20 percent.

Sources: FAO 1998; Quisumbing 1996.

Table 2: Percentage of Female-Owned Enterprises, by Sector and Size, Selected African Countries

Country/Year of survey	Sector of enterprise					Size of enterprise				Total of enterprises	Years in business	
	Textile	Agrofood	Other manuf.	Services	Other	Micro (1–9)	Small (10–49)	Medium (50–99)	Large (100+)		Female	Male
Angola 2006		40	10	29	30	25	25			25	7.8	7.6
Botswana 2006			58	56		56	54			55	9.2	9.3
Burundi 2006			21	22	39	31	42			33	8.2	7.9
Congo, Dem. Rep. of 2006	46	7	8	25	26	25	17			22	7.8	10.4
Egypt 2006	21	25	20			19	19	22	24	21	21.9	21.3
Ethiopia 2002	14	11	10			11	12			11	19.5	13.2
Madagascar 2005	48	22	12				21		24	24	14.0	17.0
Mauritania 2006			6	20	11	16	20			17	7.8	9.7
Morocco 2004	8	2	2				5	8	7	6		
Namibia 2006			17	45	19	41	32			37	9.7	11.0
South Africa 2003	15	3	10				12	7	8	9	15.3	21.0
Tanzania 2003		9	6			3	10			8	25.2	15.7
Uganda 2006	38	38	16	41		31	30			32	12.3	10.8

Source: Enterprise Survey data (various years) in World Bank/World Economic Forum/African Development Bank 2007. The figures represent the percentage of women entrepreneurs within each group. Figures are not shown when the sample size is less than 30 enterprises.

BOX 2   **Women Work Longer Hours Than Do Men**

In 1995, the United Nations Development Programme Human Development Report calculated that women's total share of work in all economic
activities accounted for more than half (53%) of all productive activity, but
within this, paid market activities represented only one-third of their
work—this compared with three-fourths of men's work in paid activities.
As a result, men receive the lion's share of income and recognition for their
economic contribution; women's work on the other hand often remains
unrecognized and undervalued.

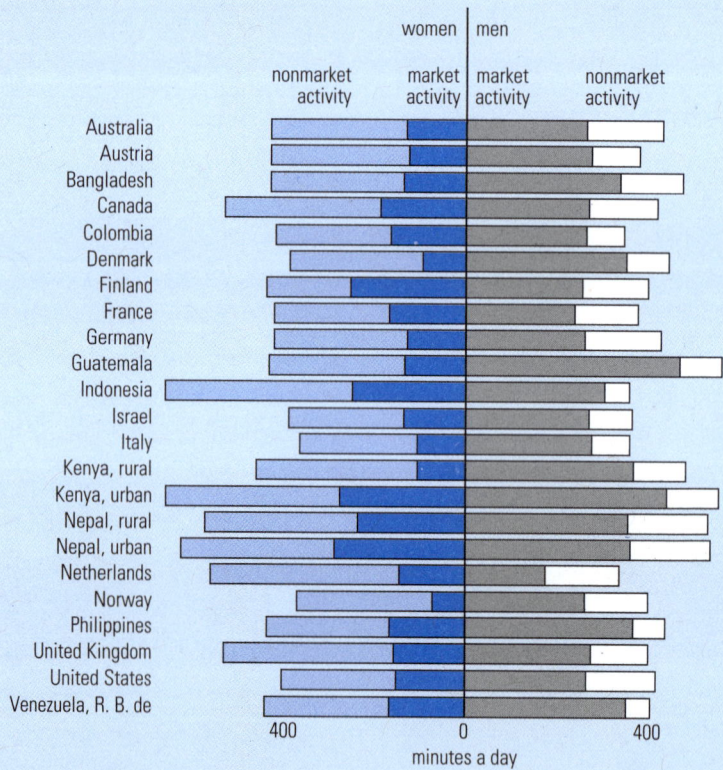

women | men

nonmarket activity | market activity | market activity | nonmarket activity

Australia
Austria
Bangladesh
Canada
Colombia
Denmark
Finland
France
Germany
Guatemala
Indonesia
Israel
Italy
Kenya, rural
Kenya, urban
Nepal, rural
Nepal, urban
Netherlands
Norway
Philippines
United Kingdom
United States
Venezuela, R. B. de

400   0   400
minutes a day

Source: UNDP 1995.

---

the time costs) disproportionately benefit women. Consequently, lowering women's
disproportionate burden of unpaid work, by prioritizing investment in infrastructure and labor-saving technologies and enacting employment and welfare policies
that facilitate more equal domestic burden sharing between men and women, is key
to widening business opportunities for women.

Checklist of Key Questions and Information Sources

- In which sectors do women and men, respectively, typically invest and work?
- What type of firms do women and men tend to run?
  - large/medium/small/micro
  - formal/informal
  - location, for example, rural/urban
  - years in operation
  - management structure
  - legal form, for example, incorporated/unincorporated
- What information exists on the nonmarket workloads of men and women and their implications for economic and business activity?
- Are women and men located in different parts of the supply chain?

Sources of Information

- National statistics
- Enterprise Surveys (www.enterprisesurveys.org)
- Household surveys, including, where available, time-use modules
- Surveys of micro and small enterprises
- Foreign Investment Advisory Service (FIAS) informality surveys
- Data from chambers of commerce and business associations
- Time-use surveys and case studies of men's and women's workloads with respect to domestic and economic activities

If published reports do not include gender-disaggregated data, the raw data behind the report may be available for analysis.

1.1.3 Identify Key Differences in Access to, and Control of, Economic Assets and Resources

Men and women differ in ownership of, access to, and control of resources. This includes land and property, access to finance, education and literacy levels, knowledge, information and training, and skills in business, management, and marketing. It also includes differences in opportunities and capacities for decision making, as reflected in women's low levels of representation in business associations, legislatures, and management and boards of private sector companies. Analysis of men's and women's economic roles, for example, is likely to show that women are more present in the informal sector. Wage gaps persist throughout the world, as discussed in the introductory chapter. A full analysis of these issues is beyond the scope of an investment climate diagnostic, but a basic understanding of this context is important for investment climate reform and for possible focused capacity-building activities.

The Beijing Platform for Action endorses a target of having at least 30 percent of decision-making positions held by women. This benchmark is seen as the minimum level at which women feel confident in participating in decision-making processes and for them to have an impact.

1.2 View Investment Climate Reform within the Broader Social and Cultural Context

Checklist of Key Questions

- Do men and women have equal land and property rights?
- Do men and women have equal access to finance?
- What differences exist between men and women in education and literacy levels?
- How well are men and women represented in the legislature, business associations, private sector management, and boards?

Sources of Information

- National statistics
- Enterprise Surveys (www.enterprisesurveys.org)
- Household surveys, including, where available, time-use modules
- Surveys of micro and small enterprises and financial institutions
- Data from chambers of commerce, business associations, and the private sector
- CEDAW reports and "shadow" reports
- Focus group discussions (FGDs) and interviews with women in business (business forums)

Although it may not be possible or appropriate in the context of an investment climate analysis to undertake a full assessment of gender relations, some understanding of the broader social and cultural environment is essential to develop workable solutions. Where traditional cultural values and informal rules inhibit women's ability to participate in the economy, reforms, however beneficial in intent, may have limited impact. Prevailing customs, beliefs, and attitudes (of women as well as of men) often confine and restrict the scope and acceptability of women's activities. In addition, a cultural environment of male dominance and decision making limits women's ability to control the revenue generated by their businesses.[2]

In some contexts men may be seen as having "public sphere" responsibilities, with women having, and being confined to, "private sphere" domestic responsibilities. Participatory poverty analyses in Kenya and Uganda show how deep-rooted is male reluctance to accept women as economically independent agents.[3] In the Middle East and North Africa Region, labor and other laws restrict the hours women may work and the type of work they may do, or require them to obtain

---

Checklist of Key Issues

- Women are likely to have had less education and are more likely than men to be illiterate.
- Women are often "time poor," shouldering the double burden of economic activity as well as domestic responsibilities.
- Women are often highly constrained in their ability to travel because of both domestic responsibilities and the need to obtain permission from husbands or other male figures.
- Women may be unable to mix with men outside their family and household.
- Women may be regarded as property or as minors who are prohibited from entering into commercial transactions without a husband or male relative's consent.
- Women frequently suffer from domestic violence.

Sources of Information

- Country studies and time-use surveys
- Reports of academic and research institutions
- Participatory Poverty Assessments
- Poverty and Social Assessments
- Country studies by international nongovernmental organizations (NGOs), and academic or research institutions
- Country CEDAW reports, including "shadow" CEDAW reports prepared by NGOs
- Country gender assessments
- Focus group discussions, forums of businesswomen
- Proverbs, stories, interviews

male permission to travel or to obtain a passport (Nabli and Chamlou 2004).[4] In the business environment, this leads to the perception that women are not "serious" as business people and therefore can be treated dismissively by financial institutions or other service providers. Such restrictions may not always be found in formal laws and regulations, and may not be identified if one only looks at business-related laws. A broader look at the legal environment, as discussed in section 1.3, is required. Sociocultural factors, though often perceived as outside the frame of reference of investment climate reform work, are elemental forces shaping the environment in which women operate and consequently deserve particular and rigorous attention in addressing the gender dimensions of investment climate reform. Conventional investment climate reform advisory projects may not be able to address these complex social and cultural issues directly; therefore, reform projects need to be designed cognizant of these issues and where they might affect intended outcomes.

1.3   Analyze the Legal Status of Men and Women

Many countries have entered into international commitments to gender equality (see annex A). But international obligations normally require domestic legislation to bring them into effect, and frequently domestic laws are not in full compliance with international equality obligations.

A country's constitution or other overarching law can contain provisions relating to gender equality to a greater or lesser extent (box 3). However, as with international commitments, laws that do not comply with constitutional guarantees of equality may exist. Moreover, equality provisions may not extend to private transactions, such as credit applications. Thus, international and constitutional guarantees of equality may have limited direct effects, although the obligation to comply with them, alongside other gender equality commitments a country has made (discussed in section 2.3), can be an important driver for reform.

When analyzing laws and regulations that affect women's economic participation, it is critical to pay attention to those that both directly (business registration, labor law) and indirectly (family law, inheritance law) affect women's capacity to participate in the private sector. In addition, especially in common law jurisdictions, "judge-made" case law can be instructive about prevailing attitudes to women's economic empowerment. In some common law countries, women's groups are seeking to use strategic litigation to "push the boundaries" and challenge legal provisions that discriminate against women.

In the Middle East, for example, a recent report noted that business and economic laws are not a problem for women entrepreneurs, but that other laws are (Chamlou 2008). Understanding the business environment for women entrepreneurs requires examining how laws are applied in the context of norms that ascribe particular roles to women (box 4).

BOX 3	Constitutional Gender-Equality Provisions in Selected African Countries

Uganda's constitution provides for equality between men and women and for affirmative action where such equality does not exist.

Kenya's constitution also provides for gender equality, but exempts from its nondiscrimination provisions "members of a particular tribe or race" with respect to the application of their customary law. Customary law is administered by traditional leaders (for example, elders) and local authorities (government appointed chiefs), and under the Judicature Act may also be applied in the formal court system in so far as it is "applicable and is not repugnant to justice and morality or inconsistent with any written law."

Swaziland has ratified international conventions (CEDAW and the Women's Rights Protocol to the African Charter on Human and Peoples' Rights), and its constitution provides for equality between genders and recognizes women's property rights. However, the customary law prohibits women from owning land or entering into a contract without a male relative's consent. Even with consent a woman lacks legal personality, so she cannot register as the title owner of a deed. The constitution states that a woman shall not be compelled to "undergo or uphold" any custom she opposes, but enforcement is problematic.

Source: Authors' research of constitutional provisions and customary law.

BOX 4	Family and Business in the Middle East

In the **Middle East** all constitutions identify the family, rather than the individual, as the central unit of society. Preserving the family is an important duty of the state, which guarantees and protects the family through its authority and institutions. Without exception, constitutions based on the family (inside and outside the region) consider the man as the main breadwinner and the head of the family and the woman as a wife and mother—relying on traditional gender roles and gender-based divisions of labor. These constitutions treat women's economic role as unnecessary or secondary. This approach often translates into overprotective laws or gendered legal interpretations in cases of ambiguities. Obedience laws, for example, which are outside business legislation, obligate women to obey their husbands. In most cases a woman's disobedience can be grounds for divorce and loss of child custody. A host of other laws aims to ensure the

(Continued)

BOX 4   **Family and Business in the Middle East (*Continued*)**

husband's authority over the family and his wife, for example, requiring women to obtain the permission of husbands to work, obtain passports, or travel. Requiring permission to obtain passports or travel is a significant impediment to doing business. Obtaining a loan can be harder as well. Although banking laws do not discriminate against female borrowers, the practice of banks across many countries is to ask for the husband as a cosigner, even if he lacks the financial resources or is not involved in the venture. The intent is to ensure that the woman's actions do not interfere with the wishes of the family or her husband.

Source: Chamlou 2008.

Checklist of Key Questions

- Which international treaty obligations does the country have in relation to gender equality?
- To what extent have these obligations been incorporated into domestic law?
- What does the country's constitution or other overarching law say about equality between genders?
- If the constitution provides for equality between genders, how is this provision operationalized in the underlying legal framework?
- Are there any exceptions to a constitutional equality provision, for example, allowing customary law to prevail in some circumstances?
- Are there laws that discriminate against women in relation to family, marriage, and property or inheritance rights; age of majority; or ability to travel?
- In a common law country, is there recent case law on women's rights, for instance, property rights?
- Are there parallel legal systems, for example, religious or customary law? If so, how do they treat relations between genders?

Sources of Information

- Ministry of foreign affairs (international commitments)
- Ministry of justice or legal databases (constitutional and legislative framework); lawyers specializing in gender issues (for example, the local branch of FIDA-International Federation of Women Lawyers)
- Reports of international NGOs on women's rights
- Country reports on CEDAW and "shadow" CEDAW reports

1.4 Identify Laws, Regulations, Procedures, and Business Obstacles That Are Perceived Differently by Men and Women

Tools to identify investment climate constraints need to capture those that have impact on women as well as those that affect men. Some constraints may affect men's and women's businesses differently, and surveys need to be designed to capture these differences. For example, the World Bank recently undertook a survey in eight Middle East and North Africa countries. Constraints that affected women, but not men, included inability to enter a business registration office without a male relative, travel without male permission, or check into a hotel on their own.[5]

Some constraints may limit both women and men but have a disproportionate impact on one or the other. For example, there is evidence that women are more likely to suffer from harassment and requests for bribes when interacting with public officials than their male counterparts. A study in India found that women had to wait on average 37 percent longer than men to see the same local government official. Women of roughly the same income as men were three times more likely to be "queue-jumped," and 16 percent of women reported sexual harassment from local government officials.[6] A survey in Bangladesh found that government officials were more likely to target female applicants for informal "speed payments" because they were assumed to have a male provider.[7] In the Arab Republic of Egypt, constraints appear in sometimes surprising ways (box 5).

BOX 5   **Egypt—Subtle Gender Differences in Investment Climate Constraints**

There are some gender-related differences in **Egypt**'s investment climate. Egyptian female-owned firms are more likely than male-owned firms to perceive access to land and electricity as problems. This finding is confirmed by additional analysis, which substantiates differences for electricity through the objective occurrence of problems. Egyptian female-owned firms report a yearly average of 14 days of interruption from power outages or surges from the public grid, compared with 10 days reported by male-owned firms. It is difficult to explain the root causes. More interesting is that female-owned firms report higher losses because of these problems (7 percent of total sales, compared with 5 percent for male-owned firms). Egyptian female-owned firms also report higher legal constraints. This difference, though not statistically significant, is confirmed by the occurrence of objective obstacles. On average, female-owned firms need 86 weeks to resolve disputes over overdue payments, eight months longer than the 54 weeks for male-owned firms. That difference is statistically significant.

Source: Chamlou 2008.

Even where there is no explicit legal or regulatory restriction, cultural or economic factors may force women to depend on men to act as intermediaries with state officials. As a result, women's interactions with officials are less efficient and women's choice is restricted.[8]

Sources for gender-disaggregated data on investment climate constraints include World Bank Enterprise Surveys, household surveys, FIAS informality surveys, data from chambers of commerce and business associations (particularly women's business associations), data from national and international NGOs involved in promoting women in private sector development, IFC Voices of Women Entrepreneurs reports, and ILO Reports.[9]

World Bank Enterprise Surveys and other data sources allow policy makers to address the extent to which investment climate constraints, such as those captured in the Doing Business reports, are perceived in the same way, or differently, by men's and women's businesses. Where such differences exist, further probing will be necessary to understand why and to develop solutions, for example, if the problem relates to women's interaction with male officials. Table 3 illustrates, for the same

---

Checklist of Key Issues

When *developing* new survey instruments:
- Ensure that women as well as men are involved in question formulation and that thought is given to identifying specific constraints that may affect one gender or the other
- Ensure male-female balance in survey sample groups—pilot and final

When *analyzing* survey results:
- Which investment climate constraints are perceived in the same way, or differently, by men's and women's businesses?
- What is the relative priority that women and men put on addressing different investment climate constraints?
- Are there constraints that are specific to women?

Sources of Information

- Enterprise Surveys (World Bank); World Economic Forum Gender Gap reports
- Global Entrepreneurship Monitor reports
- CEDAW reports
- Reports of national and international NGOs on the status of women
- Interviews and focus groups with business associations and organizations

Table 3: Entrepreneurs Identifying Selected Obstacles as Major or Severe, by Gender

Country/Year of survey	Obstacle											
	Access to land		Skills		Corruption		Crime, theft, disorder		Labor regulations		Licenses and permits	
	F	M	F	M	F	M	F	M	F	M	F	M
Angola 2006	15	26	10	22	22	37	27	35	3	12	31	31
Botswana 2006	31	23	18	14	23	22	14	22	5	9	16	16
Burundi 2006	29	30	12	10	24	14	21	17	0	2	16	10
Congo, Dem. Rep. of 2006	24	15	14	15	18	18	30	20	14	12	31	25
Egypt, Arab Rep. of 2006	29	20	35	36	59	63	·	·	24	31	14	11
Ethiopia 2002	61	63	14	15	46	43	8	11	0	4	3	10
Madagascar 2005	18	22	32	27	41	48	42	35	19	10	14	14
Mauritania 2006	14	29	26	15	21	15	0	4	0	3	2	4
Morocco 2004	38	45	36	20	16	16	9	8	18	15	18	19
Namibia 2006	19	14	13	24	26	18	26	26	9	10	9	7
South Africa 2003	6	3	19	30	19	16	35	32	16	33	0	3
Tanzania 2003		29		29		54		29		13		30
Uganda 2006	13	22	9	9	25	20	15	14	1	2	8	16

Source: Enterprise Survey data (various years) in World Bank/WEF/AfDB 2007. The figures represent percentages.

countries included in table 2, some of the areas in which men and women perceive investment climate obstacles differently.

Usually no one obstacle is commonly perceived as a constraint by all women entrepreneurs, nor is there any one country where all obstacles are perceived by women entrepreneurs as a constraint. Consequently, country- and sector-specific analysis is necessary to better understand which constraints are binding, to whom, and in which circumstances. Where published reports do not include gender-disaggregated data, the raw survey data may be available for analysis.

1.5   Ensure Women's Voices Are Heard and Issues Facing Women in Business Are Raised

Gender-aware diagnostics of the legal and regulatory environment need to be conducted in close collaboration with key women's associations, civil society groups, the business community, and government counterparts. In addition to identifying gender barriers to growth and investment, carrying out this work in an explicitly gender-inclusive manner can help build local understanding of gender and private sector development issues and strengthen the ability of local associations and civil society groups to advocate effectively for change to advance gender-sensitive reforms. Ensuring that women's voices are heard in the diagnostic process—and concomitantly in solution design, implementation, and M&E—will increase women's ability to benefit from and contribute to economic growth. An improved business-enabling environment for female-owned businesses will result in greater numbers of more successful women entrepreneurs and increased job creation.

Data collection and outreach to women need to be conducted in a way that addresses specific limitations that sometimes affect women (box 6).

One approach to engaging women in the diagnostic and solution design phases is "women-in-business" forums, which give women an opportunity to articulate success factors and challenges to entrepreneurship. This approach was at the core of the diagnostic work undertaken in the South Pacific in February–March 2009 (box 7).

Gender inclusion can also lead to a better understanding of the underlying hard data and their implications for the business environment. For instance, it is difficult to distinguish between business ownership and business management using available business registration or survey data. This is especially important in the case of family-run businesses—and many women's businesses, especially in Africa, are family businesses.[10] When shares are registered in the names of both husband and wife, the extent to which ownership is truly "joint" cannot be ascertained easily. Similar issues arise with respect to management and decision making in family businesses. Such issues can be uncovered in focus groups, women-in-business forums, and public-private dialogue mechanisms.

BOX 6	Using Appropriate Data Collection Methods to Reach Women

Appropriate data collection methods need to be used when seeking information from women in the course of a diagnostic. Data collection methods should take into account the likelihood of the following:

- Women often have lower literacy levels (for example, for completing survey forms).
- Middle-class urban women are not necessarily representative of women generally.
- Women are less likely to speak at public meetings (for example, in mixed-gender focus groups).
- Women may not be able to attend meetings, either because of time poverty, social barriers, or denial of permission by husband.
- Women entrepreneurs are often not well represented in membership-based private sector associations.

BOX 7	Dialogue with Businesswomen: Diagnostic and Solution Design

During an IFC diagnostic mission in the **South Pacific** reviewing the scope for incorporation of gender in the IFC's investment climate reform initiatives, IFC initiated women's business forums in Papua New Guinea, Samoa, the Solomon Islands, and Tonga. Where possible, forums were organized using the offices of existing women's business organizations (for example, the Solomon Islands Women in Business Association). But in Papua New Guinea, where the women's business association was perceived to be weak and fairly unrepresentative, invitations were sent out to businesswomen through a variety of means. In Tonga the forum was organized by the advisory team implementing the regulatory simplification project, whereas in Samoa the forum was organized through the dynamic leadership of the Small Business Enterprise Centre.

Forums were informal, with the clear objective for the women to share stories of the constraints they face related to the investment climate and with a view to influencing IFC programs to address women's concerns. In the Solomon Islands and Papua New Guinea, as an ice-breaker, women were asked to share in pairs what they "loved" about being in business and what they "hated"—and answers were pinned up on the walls.

(Continued)

> **BOX 7** **Dialogue with Businesswomen: Diagnostic and Solution Design (*Continued*)**
>
> Networking and forming relationships came out as key positives. In breakout groups, women who had encountered problems in particular areas (for example, business start-up or dispute resolution) were asked to provide details, using the questionnaires in this *Practitioners' Guide.* The session ended with a prioritization exercise, with participants voting on which solutions to problems encountered were the most important to take forward.
>
> Feedback from the forums indicated the women appreciated the chance to network and share common concerns; many business cards were exchanged. In Papua New Guinea, it is hoped that the forum can develop into an ongoing mechanism for businesswomen and feed into new structures being developed for public-private dialogue (PPD). In the Solomon Islands, the forum was an opportunity to strengthen the existing Women in Business Association and to encourage new members to join. In Samoa, the forum was seen as a useful starting point for strengthening women's engagement in existing mechanisms of dialogue with the government, and, possibly, helping to establish the foundations for a future public-private dialogue initiative.
>
> *Source:* Based on authors' field research.

Further, as there may be differences in opportunities and capacity for men and women to influence economic decision making—as reflected by women's usually low levels of representation in business associations, legislatures, and boards and management of private sector companies—an inclusive approach to fact-finding will ensure that women's voices are heard and issues are brought to the attention of policy makers, which otherwise might not be the case.

Checklist of Key Issues

- Use data collection methods that are appropriate for women.
- Consider women-in-business forums or other mechanisms aimed at giving women opportunity to voice their concerns and to identify critical success factors and obstacles affecting their business.
- Use business forums and conduct individual interviews with women, alongside analysis by local experts, which are useful means of identifying and tackling constraining social and cultural issues.
- Use "profiles" of women in business to highlight specific investment climate issues faced by women.
- Be clear about whether the questions are aimed at the business manager or owner.
- In the case of a family-run business, seek to determine what the relationship is between ownership and management and whether men or women are the final decision makers in the business.

Step 2   Solution Design

2.1   Test Political/Cultural Acceptability and Create a Conducive Environment for Reform

In some countries, gender is high on the political agenda. In others, it is much more difficult to address gender issues overtly. Country circumstances matter. For instance, following the genocide in Rwanda, women were seen as "the main agents of reconstruction." The government explicitly adopted a policy of gender equality, amending the country's constitution and legal framework to reflect this. In 2007, Rwanda was ranked as the third most equitable country in the world (after Sweden and Finland).[11] In other countries, reforms to improve the position of women may hit deep-rooted opposition. In Uganda a clause in the Land Act 1998 to give married women coownership of matrimonial land was "lost" and did not appear in the final version of the act, despite having been approved by the parliament. Successive attempts since then to reinstate the lost clause have stalled.

Signatories to international treaties on gender equality, through their treaty reporting requirements, have opened themselves up to international scrutiny on their compliance with their obligations. This can be a lever for reform (box 8).

Some reforms have the potential to be of particular benefit to women but will also benefit men, for example, simplifying business entry (because women tend to be less well placed than men to deal with complex entry processes). Such "gender blind" reforms may be more politically acceptable. The diagnostic work should identify and prioritize the issues that are most likely to benefit women.

Sociocultural issues can be addressed carefully in women's business forums, in direct interviews with stakeholders, or as part of the public-private dialogue, where

---

BOX 8   Compliance with CEDAW and Reporting Requirements

CEDAW commits signatory countries to submit regular reports to the CEDAW Committee at the United Nations (UN) on their compliance with their treaty obligations. NGOs will frequently submit a "shadow" report critiquing the formal report.

For example, the Government of **Vanuatu**'s 2004 national report on their compliance with CEDAW submitted to the UN highlights ongoing gender inequalities in its legal framework. NGOs in Vanuatu published a "shadow" CEDAW report at the same time, further highlighting these issues and making the case for reform.

Sources: CEDAW 2004; IWRAW-AP 2007.

women can identify the most important issues as well as any culturally appropriate actions for tackling them.

2.2 Involve Women As Well As Men in Developing Appropriate Solutions

Stakeholders to involve in developing solutions and testing proposed solutions include

- government or other body responsible for defining and implementing investment climate reforms;
- government agency responsible for gender equity (usually a ministry for women's affairs or for gender);
- women's business associations and women in business; and
- gender technical specialists (for example, in government, NGOs, or the donor community).

Bringing stakeholders together to support gender-responsive reforms was carried out in Indonesia by the State Ministry of Women's Empowerment partnering with the Indonesian Women's Business Association (box 9).

BOX 9   Stakeholder Engagement in Indonesia

Although women in **Indonesia** owned 60 percent of the country's formal and informal micro, small, and medium enterprises, they were often denied credit without approval from their husbands. This was one of many paradoxes the IFC sought to highlight through a public outreach campaign aimed at increasing awareness of women's role in business. Two stakeholders, the State Ministry of Women's Empowerment and the Indonesian Women's Business Association, were critical to the campaign and to future reform efforts. The project team dedicated six months to presenting its research findings and building consensus with the two stakeholders on messages, facts, figures, and issues to be communicated. The team sought to tap into the deep understanding of existing perceptions and local support for the endeavor in order to understand the sociocultural environment, draw on the experiences of local stakeholders to gather input, develop strategies to ensure that the issue would be addressed effectively, ensure messages would resonate among target audiences, and unleash women's economic potential. The campaign drew on two research publications with overtly different approaches:

(Continued)

> **BOX 9** **Stakeholder Engagement in Indonesia (*Continued*)**
>
> - *Access to Credit for Businesswomen in Indonesia* showcased analytical findings to be leveraged in policy discussions or distilled for general audiences.
> - *Voices of Women in the Private Sector* presented stories of women entrepreneurs that a wider audience could understand and with which they could empathize.
>
> Both approaches were important to the project's dual goals of encouraging policy responsiveness and raising public awareness. Survey findings can be used by the policy community that will eventually be critical to supporting and pushing through the reforms to improve the business climate for women. Communicating similar information through anecdotes and individual stories will more likely gain the interest of a broader audience base.
>
> *Source:* Adapted from World Bank 2007.

2.3   Link with Existing Reform Strategies of the Government

Experience suggests that for gender to be successfully incorporated within an investment climate reform program, institutional responsibility needs to lie with the government entity in charge of investment policy and private sector development.[12] It is best to work with government or other bodies that have line responsibility for investment climate reform. In some cases, having active "champions" of gender issues within public policy-making agencies is especially helpful. For example, in Uganda the female head of the Uganda Investment Authority championed women in business and drove forward investment climate reforms specifically aimed at benefiting women.

In other cases, the process can be a tool for advocating the incorporation of gender. The government of Kenya's Private Sector Development Strategy explicitly recognizes the need to mainstream gender. Gender is now being incorporated within the action plans being developed under the strategy.

Many countries have a national gender or women's policy, strategy, or action plan, in which their commitments to gender equality, including the Millennium Development Goals (MDGs), their compliance with CEDAW, their implementation of the Beijing Platform for Action, and measures undertaken in the framework of regional charters and other national policy frameworks are specified. In supporting gender-responsive reform, it will be important to develop solutions that support, and are compatible with, national gender policy. It will also be essential to facilitate or strengthen partnerships between economic management agencies and those institutions within government (usually a ministry with responsibility for women or gender) that are responsible for implementing the country's gender strategy and its commitments to gender equality.

Partnerships between investment climate reformers and gender policy makers can be strengthened in several ways—including through

- capacity building for gender experts on investment climate reform and investment climate reform experts on gender issues;
- developing structures that include both groups, for example, advocacy coalitions, joint meetings of donor gender and private sector development working groups, steering and technical committees that include both genders, and private sector development government institutions; and
- inclusion of both sides, and the private sector, in PPD forums and other mechanisms of dialogue.

Consideration should be given to including gender specialists on investment climate reform program's implementation structures—for example, on steering and technical committees, and in any team of technical experts. The government ministry or agency with responsibility for gender or women should, if possible, be involved—although capacity building may be necessary.

2.4 Draw on In-Country Resources and Expertise

Just as many countries have articulated gender strategies, so, too, do they have valuable sources of information and expertise on gender issues. In developing solutions for gender-aware investment climate reform, drawing on local, or locally based, expertise can help provide relevant information and ideas, as much in the diagnostic phase as solution design. Some countries have university departments, faculties, think tanks, and research institutions focused on gender issues. In many countries multilateral and bilateral agencies have gender desks. These work with government counterparts to prepare diagnostic studies in key areas, as is the case with United Nations Development Fund for Women's Situation Analyses of Women, UNDP's National Human Development Reports, Country Gender Assessments from the World Bank and other multilateral development banks, and country-focused work in global reports, such as the Progress of the World's Women reports, Global Enterprise Monitor reports, and others.

Step 3   Implementation and M&E

3.1   Establish Baselines

The critical importance of monitoring and evaluation in program design and implementation is well recognized. The approach to M&E builds on the core indicators developed by IFC and on the 2008 Monitoring and Evaluation Handbook. These tools have not, to date, explicitly focused on gender-relevant or gender-disaggregated indicators except to a certain extent.[13] Some of the broader issues affecting the design and implementation of M&E systems have important gender dimensions (box 10).

BOX 10   Key Dimensions of Monitoring and Evaluation: Gender Perspective

- **Results are differentiated by type of business.** The M&E framework needs to recognize that impacts of investment climate reforms may differ by category of business, depending on size, sector of operation, location, and other characteristics, including gender, age, and socioeconomic background of owner or operator. Gender is a universal dimension of diversity, and, often, a dimension of disadvantage. Capturing these different dimensions of diversity is one of the key tasks of the M&E framework.
- **Results are affected by factors beyond conventional investment climate work.** Interventions not typically labeled as investment climate—such as education improvements, legal reforms not directly related to the business environment, sociocultural changes, and political reform—make important contributions to improved economic development, and their impact cannot be easily distinguished from investment climate interventions. This is especially the case with respect to gender, where broader factors, addressed in the diagnostic phase, differentially affect the capacity of men and women to start and operate a business and engage in economic transactions. A gender-focused M&E framework needs to address some of these broader factors and track the changes that are likely to have the greatest impact on women in business.
- **Indicators take many forms.** There are several types of indicators, including direct/indirect, qualitative/quantitative, process-focused, and cross-cutting indicators. According to the Monitoring and Evaluation Handbook, the experience of women registering businesses may best

(Continued)

> **BOX 10** **Key Dimensions of Monitoring and Evaluation: Gender Perspective (*Continued*)**
>
> be captured through qualitative and process-focused indicators. While such indicators are often perceived as more subjective and consequently less reliable than quantitative indicators, they are, as the handbook points out, important means of addressing diversity and inclusion, which are, in turn, critical elements of a gender-focused framework.
>
> - **Inclusion and participation of stakeholders are key.** The handbook stresses the value and usefulness of participatory M&E. Clearly identifying stakeholders and champions of reform, and interacting with these stakeholders in designing and implementing M&E, are key factors both to define appropriate and relevant indicators and to ensure ownership of the entire process. This is especially relevant for gender-focused work and needs to be at the core of the M&E effort.
>
> *Source:* Authors, based on the *M&E Handbook* (IFC 2008).

For all three dimensions of the module—core diagnostic, solution design, and M&E—it is important to collect baseline data from which change and progress can be measured. Baselines are especially important from a gender standpoint because it is essential to understand the starting point for gender-responsive reforms and to reveal from the outset the ways in which a gender perspective can inform the reform effort. Analysis in each of the submodules presented previously can be expected to provide country-level baseline data and indicators covering broader economic, legal and regulatory, and sociocultural dimensions that are needed both to define the reform areas to prioritize and to measure changes in key areas of reform. Clearly, not all these data will be available, or easily obtainable, in every country context, and some trade-offs in terms of coverage and effort required may have to be made. Nonetheless, in many countries much of this information will be available from in-country or international (UN, ILO) sources and can provide the essential underpinnings for measuring change. Annex B tabulates the core baseline indicators in each of the areas covered in this module. M&E issues specific to each of the eight modules of this guide will be addressed in the respective modules.

3.2 Integrate Gender-Focused Indicators into Reform Program M&E Systems

There are clearly identifiable gender dimensions to the core indicators with which IFC/FIAS measures performance of investment climate programs. These core indicators and their gender dimensions are summarized in table 4. These core indicators can be integrated into investment climate reform programs with appropriate adaptations to the specific circumstances and priorities of a given country program.

In addition, other factors relating to institutional responsiveness to women, gender differences in information and knowledge about reforms undertaken, and, in some circumstances, additional sociocultural limitations on women can be expected to affect men's and women's ability to participate in, and benefit from, investment climate reforms. Data gathering in these areas is needed to form part of the baseline against which to measure changes in institutional performance and changes in women's access to the benefits reform brings. These are summarized in table 5.

Table 4: Gender Focus of Core M&E Indicators

OUTPUT INDICATORS	
Core indicator	Gender focus (Gender-disaggregation)
Number of entities receiving advisory services	• Disaggregate business entities by gender of business owner where feasible • Track inclusion of women's business associations receiving assistance • Determine ratio of men to women beneficiaries in the entities receiving assistance
Number of reports (assessments, manuals) completed	• Number of reports with gender-disaggregated data • Number of assessments addressing gender issues • Number of legal or other gender-focused reviews undertaken
Number of procedures/practices proposed for improvement or elimination	• Number of procedures addressing gender-specific barriers • Number of procedures with anticipated gender-specific impacts
Number of new laws, regulations, codes, and amendments drafted or submitted for drafting	• Number of gender-responsive laws, regulations, and so forth drafted • Number of gender-responsive provisions in new laws, regulations, and so forth
Number of participants in training events, workshops, conferences, and so on	• Number of men and women participants in these events • Number of women-focused events
Number of participants providing feedback on satisfaction	• Number and/or percentage of men and women providing feedback on satisfaction
Number of participants reporting "satisfied" or "very satisfied" with workshops, training, seminars, conferences, and so on	• Number and/or percentage of men and women reporting "satisfied" or "very satisfied" with these events
Number of media appearances	• Number of men and women representing the media • Extent to which gender issues are addressed in media appearances
OUTCOME INDICATORS	
Number of recommended laws, regulations, codes, and amendments enacted	• Number of gender-responsive laws, regulations, and so on enacted • Number of gender-responsive provisions in laws, regulations, and so on enacted
Number of recommended procedures/practices improved or eliminated	• Number of procedures addressing gender-specific barriers improved or eliminated • Number of procedures with anticipated gender-specific impacts improved or eliminated

(Continued)

Table 4: Gender Focus of Core M&E Indicators (*Continued*)

Average number of days to comply with business regulation	• Number of days disaggregated by gender of business owner
Average official cost to comply with business regulation	• Cost disaggregated by gender of business owner (to capture corruption or other differences)
Number of entities that implemented recommended changes	• Number of entities disaggregated by gender of business owner, where possible
IMPACT INDICATORS	
Value of aggregate private sector savings from recommended changes	• Value disaggregated by gender of business owner
Value of investment financing facilitated by advisory services	• Disaggregated investment flows, by gender of business owner
Number of formal jobs created	• Number of formal jobs created, disaggregated by gender and by sector

Table 5: Gender Baselines on Institutional Performance, Knowledge, and Other Factors

Data required	Gender focus (Gender-disaggregation)	Source of data
Agency performance		
• Agency operation and accessibility • Online registration	• Opening hours of registration, licensing, or other agency considerations • Accessible and safe location • Welcoming of women • Percentage of men and women managers and staff in the agency • Percentage of men and women with access to Internet	• FGDs • Agency management • Women-in-business forums • Business associations
Knowledge of reforms		
• Knowledge of entry requirements and procedures • Knowledge of licensing requirements • Knowledge of legal (alternative dispute resolution) procedures	• Ascertain state of knowledge of both men and women of these requirements and procedures	• FGDs • Agency management • Women-in-business forums • Business associations • Informality surveys
Mobility restrictions and other constraints		
• Mobility and other restrictions or limitations	• Do women have to obtain husband or male permission to obtain a passport or travel? • Do women have to obtain husband or male permission to open bank account or transact business? • Are there other gender-based restrictions on travel or networking?	• FGDs • Women's business associations • Women's legal rights • NGOs • Country legal or social analysis

Figure 1 **Integrating Gender in the M&E of Investment Climate Reform Programs**

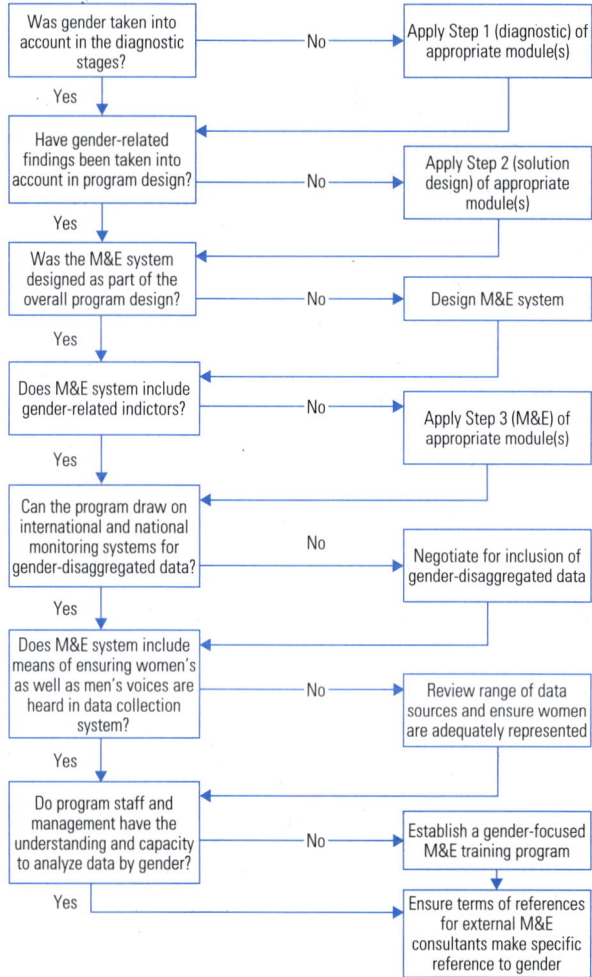

Was gender taken into account in the diagnostic stages? — No → Apply Step 1 (diagnostic) of appropriate module(s)

Yes ↓

Have gender-related findings been taken into account in program design? — No → Apply Step 2 (solution design) of appropriate module(s)

Yes ↓

Was the M&E system designed as part of the overall program design? — No → Design M&E system

Yes ↓

Does M&E system include gender-related indictors? — No → Apply Step 3 (M&E) of appropriate module(s)

Yes ↓

Can the program draw on international and national monitoring systems for gender-disaggregated data? — No → Negotiate for inclusion of gender-disaggregated data

Yes ↓

Does M&E system include means of ensuring women's as well as men's voices are heard in data collection system? — No → Review range of data sources and ensure women are adequately represented

Yes ↓

Do program staff and management have the understanding and capacity to analyze data by gender? — No → Establish a gender-focused M&E training program

Yes → Ensure terms of references for external M&E consultants make specific reference to gender

Source: Authors.

Annex A   International Treaties and Commitments

International Treaties

The **Convention on the Elimination of All Forms of Discrimination Against Women** (CEDAW) came into force in 1981. States are required to take appropriate steps in all fields to eliminate discrimination against women. Specifically, Article 13(b) addresses equality of access to credit; Article 11, equality in employment; and Article 5, equality before the law. The **Optional Protocol to CEDAW** (2000) gives women the option to demand from the committee that it review infringement of their rights (this is known as a *communication procedure*). The committee can also launch an enquiry into allegations of violations by a state of rights guaranteed by the convention (*inquiry procedure*).

The **International Labour Organization** adopted different **conventions** ratified by its member countries. They aim to tackle discrimination in the workplace, remuneration, maternity leave, and so on. For example, Convention Number 100 sets the standards for equal remuneration; Number 111 promotes equal opportunity and treatment in employment and occupation.

Examples of Regional Treaties

The **Protocol to the African Charter on Human and People's Rights on the Rights of Women in Africa** commits states to combat all forms of discrimination against women through appropriate legislative, institutional, and other measures, and to take corrective action in areas where discrimination against women in law continues to exist (Article 2). This includes equality of access to employment; equal remuneration; transparency in recruitment; paid maternity leave; the promotion of economic activities where women are overrepresented, such as the informal sector; and equal taxation treatment of women and men (Article 13).

The **Southern African Development Community Protocol on Gender and Development** adopted in 2008 contains 23 targets, including the inclusion of gender equality in all constitutions with affirmative action clauses and abolition of the legal minority status of women. There are also provisions on equal land ownership, trade, and entrepreneurship.

Other International Commitments

The **Beijing Declaration** and **Beijing Platform for Action** are the result of the Fourth World Conference on Women held in Beijing in 1995. They set out an agenda of actions to be taken to combat inequality, including in the economy, for example, in relation to employment and access to credit. Many countries have developed national plans of action to implement these commitments.

The **Cairo Program of Action** is the outcome document of the International Conference on Population and Development held in Cairo in 1994. Commitments were made in relation to gender equality and the empowerment of women, and many countries have developed national plans of action to implement these commitments.

Goal 3 of the **Millennium Development Goals (MDGs)** specifically addresses gender equality and the empowerment of women. Countries confirmed their commitment to Goal 3 in the **2005 World Summit Outcome** in the areas of education, land tenure (paragraph 58(b)), business entry, housing, reproductive health, access to labor markets and labor protection (paragraph 58(d)), and governmental institutions (paragraph 58(g)).

Annex B   Core Module Baseline Indicators and Principal Data Sources

Data required	Gender focus (Gender disaggregation)	Source of data
Economic and social data		
• Number of enterprises by sector, size, region, age, and other characteristics • Number and percentage of enterprises in formal and informal activity	• Number and percentage of enterprises by these characteristics disaggregated by gender	• World Bank Enterprise Surveys • Business registers • Business associations
• Economically active population or labor force participation and employment data by sector, region (urban and rural), occupational category, age	• Number and percentage of economically active/labor force participation disaggregated by gender	• Labor force surveys • Household surveys • Population censuses • ILO (KILM) and other data
• Number of labor force in professional and managerial positions	• Number of male and female labor force in professional and managerial positions	• Labor force surveys • Household surveys • UN data
• Number of labor force who are unpaid family workers in the informal sector	• Disaggregated by gender	• Labor force surveys • Household surveys • UN data
• Number of labor force who are working in the informal sector	• Disaggregated by gender	• Labor force surveys • Household surveys • UN data • Informality surveys
• Incidence of part-time and full-time work	• Disaggregated by gender	• Labor force surveys • Household surveys • UN data
• Time use in selected activities, including unpaid housework and child care	• Disaggregated by gender	• Time-use surveys • Time modules in household surveys (LSMS) • Specialized sources
• Education/Literacy data by age, region	• Gender disaggregated	• Administrative surveys UN system • MDG tracking
• Leadership/Public life	• Number and percentage of men and women in leadership positions: cabinet, parliament • Number and percentage of men and women in the judiciary, and in informal justice systems (ADR)	• Country data • UN data • Inter-Parliamentary Union Web site

(Continued)

Data required	Gender focus (Gender disaggregation)	Source of data
• Leadership/Private sector	• Number and percentage of men and women on corporate boards • Number and percentage of men and women in senior management • Number and percentage of men and women in business associations, chambers of commerce, or investor councils	• Businesses • Business associations • Catalyst and other similar analysis
• Child-care policies	• Number of employers providing child care • Number of children (0–3 and 3–6) in child care	
• Financial sector, banking system, and access to finance	• Number and percentage of men women accessing finance • Number and volume of loans accessed by men and women entrepreneurs	• Administrative data • Banking records • FinScope surveys • Other specialized surveys
• Salary/Wage differences among types of workers	• Disaggregated by gender	• Household surveys • Labor force surveys • Administrative data • Enterprise surveys
Data on the legal and regulatory framework		
• International instruments with focus on attention to gender	• CEDAW • ILO Conventions • Beijing Platform • MDG commitments (esp. MDG 3)	• CEDAW reports • Legal studies • Women's lawyers associations • MDG indicators/Web site
• Constitution/Overarching laws	• Is gender equality enshrined in the constitution? • Does the constitution bar discrimination on the basis of gender?	• CEDAW reports • Legal studies • Women's lawyers associations
• Family law (marriage, inheritance, and succession)	• Identification of provisions that discriminate on the basis of gender	• CEDAW reports • Legal studies • Women's lawyers associations • Gender/Doing Business legal database
• Customary law/Custom	• Identification of provisions/ practices that discriminate on the basis of gender	• CEDAW reports • Legal studies
• Employment/Labor laws	• Identification of provisions that discriminate on the basis of gender	• CEDAW reports • Legal studies • Business associations

(Continued)

Data required	Gender focus (Gender disaggregation)	Source of data
	• "Protective" provisions (health/safety) • Maternity/Paternity leave provisions	• Women's lawyers associations • Gender/Doing business legal database
• Legal and regulatory framework affecting business	• Inventory of legal and regulatory provisions that are discriminatory or otherwise differentially affect men's and women's economic capacities	• Diagnostic studies • CEDAW reports • Women's lawyers associations • Gender/Doing business legal database
• Family leave policies and percentage who avail themselves of this • Number of weeks	• Disparities in maternity and paternity leave policies • Percentage of men and women who avail themselves of this	• Government social services • Business associations • Women's lawyers associations
• Mobility and other restrictions	• Do women have to obtain husband or other male permission to obtain a passport or travel? • Do women have to obtain husband or other male permission to open a bank account or transact business?	• FGDs • Women's business associations • Women's legal rights NGOs • Country legal/social analysis

Data on social and cultural dimensions

Data required	Gender focus (Gender disaggregation)	Source of data
• Prevailing attitudes and beliefs	• Attitudes and beliefs toward women • How are businesswomen perceived?	• Proverbs • Case studies • Participatory appraisals • National/global surveys
• Perceptions of obstacles to business	• Disaggregate perceptions data by gender to determine whether and where differences exist	• Enterprise surveys • Household surveys • Specialized sector surveys • Business associations • Gender/Doing Business legal database
• Mobility and other restrictions	• Do women have to obtain husband or other male permission to obtain a passport or travel? • Do women have to obtain husband or other male permission to open a bank account or transact business?	• FGDs • Women's business associations • Women's legal rights NGOs • Country legal/social analysis • Gender/Doing Business legal database

Not all these data will be available, or easily obtainable, in every country context, and some trade-offs in terms of coverage and effort required may have to be made. In many countries much of this information will be available from in-country or international (UN, ILO) sources and can provide the essential underpinnings for measuring change.

Annex C   Checklist of Key Issues

	Sources to use
DIAGNOSTIC	
2.1. Analyze the Business Sector through a Gender Lens In which sectors do women and men, respectively, typically invest and work? Are women and men located in different parts of the supply chain? What type of firms do women and men tend to run—large/medium/small/micro, formal/informal, location (for example, rural/urban), years in operation, management structure, legal form (for example, incorporated/unincorporated)?	• National statistics and household surveys • Surveys of micro and small enterprises • FIAS informality surveys • Data from chambers of commerce and business associations
2.2 Disaggregate Investment Climate Constraints Faced by Women and Men When Developing Survey Questions: • Ensure that women as well as men are involved in question formulation and that thought is given to identifying specific constraints that may affect one gender or the other. • Ensure male-female balance in survey sample groups—pilot and final. When analyzing survey results: • Which investment climate constraints are perceived in the same way, or differently, by men's and women's businesses? • What is the relative priority that women and men put on addressing different investment climate constraints? • Are there constraints specific to women?	• Enterprise surveys • Household surveys • FIAS informality surveys • Data from chambers of commerce and business associations (particularly women's business associations)
2.3. Ensure Women's Voices Are Heard Use appropriate data collection methods for women. Be clear about whether the questions are aimed at the business manager or owner. In the case of a family-run business, determine who the "real" owner is—male or female.	
2.4. Analyze the Legal Status of Men and Women Which international treaty obligations does the country have in relation to gender equality? To what extent have these obligations been incorporated into domestic law? What does the country's constitution, or other overarching law, say about equality between genders?	• Ministry of foreign affairs (international commitments) • Ministry of justice and legal databases (constitutional and legislative framework) • Lawyers specializing in gender issues (for example, the local branch of FIDA—the international women lawyers association)

(Continued)

	Sources to use
If the constitution provides for equality between genders, how is this provision operationalized in the underlying legal framework?	• Reports of international NGOs on women's rights • Country reports on CEDAW
Are there any exceptions to a constitutional equality provision, for example, allowing customary law to prevail in some circumstances?	
Are there laws that discriminate against women in relation to family, marriage, and property or inheritance rights; age of majority; or ability to travel?	
In a common law country, is there recent case law on women's rights, for example, property rights?	
Are there parallel legal systems, for example, religious or customary law? If so, how do they treat relations between genders?	
2.5. Consider Differences in Access to Economic Resources Compare women's and men's educational levels—primary, secondary, and tertiary. Compare women's and men's access to training and skills development. Compare women's and men's participation in key decision-making bodies, including business associations, investor councils, and lobby groups (as compared with the Beijing Platform for Action's 30% target).	• National statistics on gender-disaggregated education levels • CEDAW reports • Reports of national and international NGOs on the status of women • Interviews and focus groups with business associations and organizations
2.6. View Investment Climate Reform within the Broader Social and Cultural Context Bear in mind: • Women are often likely to have had less education, and are more likely than men to be illiterate. • Women are often "time poor," shouldering the double burden of economic activity as well as domestic responsibilities. In areas where there is a high rate of HIV/AIDS, women often carry the added time and financial burden of caring for the orphans of relatives, as well as caring for sick family members. • Women are often highly constrained in their ability to travel because of both their domestic responsibilities and the need to obtain permission from their husbands. • Women may be unable to mix with men outside their family and household. • Women may be regarded as property—or as minors—unable to enter into commercial transactions without a husband's or male relative's consent. • Women frequently suffer from domestic violence.	• Country studies and time-use surveys • Reports of academic or research institutions • Participatory Poverty Assessments • Poverty and Social Assessments • Country studies by international NGOs • Academic and research institutions • CEDAW reports • Country Gender Assessments • Proverbs, stories, interviews

(Continued)

SOLUTION DESIGN

2.7. Test Political and Cultural Acceptability

Explore attitude of governments to gender reform.

Understand that gender-blind reforms that nonetheless have a disproportionate benefit for women may be more politically acceptable.

2.8. Link with Existing Strategies

Link with national gender policy and develop solutions in light of priorities set out in it.

2.9. Involve Women As Well As Men in Developing Appropriate Solutions

Include as stakeholders:

- Government agency responsible for gender equity (usually a ministry for women or for gender)
- Women's business associations
- Gender technical specialists (for example, in government, NGOs, or the donor community)

IMPLEMENTATION

3.1. Include Gender Specialists in Program Implementation Arrangements

Include gender specialists in implementation structures (for example, steering committees, technical committees, team of experts).

Include government agency responsible for gender issues, for example, ministry for women's affairs.

3.2. Make Linkages across the Gender-Investment Climate Institutional Divide

Make linkages between government, donor, and NGO organizations responsible for gender and investment climate reform, including through

- capacity building for gender experts on investment climate reform and for investment climate reform experts on gender issues; and
- structures that include both groups, such as advocacy coalitions, joint meetings, donor gender and private sector development working groups; steering and technical committees that include both gender and private sector development government institutions.

MONITORING AND EVALUATION

3.3. Gender-Disaggregate Data and Analyze Gender Differences

Disaggregate all data collected by gender.

Use surveys or perception studies to explore reasons for the differences revealed.

3.4. Link with Existing Data Collection and Gender Disaggregate

Source gender-disaggregated data in existing surveys, including the following:

- International monitoring systems: World Bank's Doing Business Survey (which is currently being updated to incorporate gender analyses), World Bank's Good Governance Survey
- National monitoring systems: poverty-reduction strategies; medium-term expenditure frameworks
- Research and academic institutions, NGOs: socioeconomic data that disaggregate between men and women are usually available.

If published reports do not contain gender-disaggregated information, raw data may be available for gender disaggregation.

(Continued)

3.5. Ensure Women's Voices Are Heard

Undertake targeted data collection from women bearing in mind the following:

- Women often have lower literacy levels (for example, for completing survey forms).
- Middle-class urban women are not necessarily representative of women generally.
- Women are less likely to speak at public meetings (for example, in mixed-gender focus groups).
- Women may not be able to attend meetings either because of their time poverty and household tasks, because it may be socially unacceptable for them to do so, or because they may not be permitted by their husbands.
- Include women's business associations in surveys. If they don't exist, consider supporting establishment.

3.6. Ensure Key Staff Understand the Gender Dimension

Train the staff in charge of implementing the program so they can understand gender issues and take them into account in the design and management phases of M&E system.

Include in Terms of References (TORs) for external M&E consultants a specific requirement for them to analyze findings by gender.

PUBLIC-PRIVATE DIALOGUE

3.7. Ensure Women Are Represented in Public-Private Dialogue Structures

Include people or organizations able to represent the concerns of women and men to public-private dialogue structures.

Involve private sector organizations as well as government agencies in charge of implementing gender policies. Include both formal and informal sectors in public-private dialogue structures.

3.8. Undertake Training and Capacity-Building Activities and Build Coalitions

Provide capacity building to existent women's advocacy organizations in order to extend their skills to investment climate issues.

Build capacity for organizations representing business interests to government in relation to gender issues.

Facilitate partnerships among organizations with technical gender expertise and private business organizations, as this allows the process of advocacy to go forward.

3.9. Incorporate Indicators That Highlight Gendered Aspects of Public-Private Dialogue

Include gender in output and outcome indicators.

Notes

1. For an overview of the issue of unpaid work and care tasks, see Budlender, "Why Should We Care about Unpaid Work" (UNDP, 2006). For a review of these issues in Africa, see Blackden and Wodon, eds., "Gender, Time Use, and Poverty in Sub-Saharan Africa" (Washington, DC: World Bank, 2006).

2. Ruiz Abril, Maria Elena, "Girls Vulnerability Assessment" (World Bank, 2008).

3. For Uganda, see "Second Participatory Poverty Assessment Report" (Kampala: Ministry of Finance, Planning, and Economic Development, 2002); "Uganda: From Periphery to Center, A Strategic Country Gender Assessment" (report No. 30136-UG,). (World Bank, 2006.) For Kenya, see "The Kenya Strategic Country Gender Assessment" (World Bank, 2003).

4. Nabli and Chamlou, *Gender and Development in the Middle East and North Africa: Women in the Public Sphere* (World Bank, 2004).

5. Chamlou, *The Environment for Women's Entrepreneurship in the Middle East and North Africa Region*, 24.

6. DFID, *The Gender Manual: A Practical Guide*, 5.

7. UNIFEM, "Who Answers to Women? Gender & Accountability," 44.

8. The extent of "male intermediation" is illustrated by the fact that more than a quarter of women in developing countries do not have a say in decisions about their own health care (Progress of the World's Women 2008/2009, UNIFEM).

9. For further information on World Bank Enterprise Surveys, see http://www.enterprisesurveys.org/. To read more about IFC's "Voices of Women Entrepreneurs" reports, see www.ifc.org/gender.

10. For a fuller treatment of gender dimensions of business ownership in Africa, see World Economic Forum, World Bank, and African Development Bank, *2007 Africa Competitiveness Report.*

11. IFC, *Rwanda: Review of the Legal and Regulatory Framework for Business from a Legal Perspective* (IFC, 2008) and IFC, *Rwanda: Voices of Women Entrepreneurs, 2008.*

12. Cutura, "Smart Lessons in Advisory Services" (IFC, 2006).

13. The core indicators do include tracking the number of women participants in workshops, training events, seminars, conferences, and so on.

Public-Private Dialogue

This Module Should be Used in Conjunction with the Core Module

Summary

MODULE 1

Introduction

Public-private dialogue (PPD) in the investment climate is the process of bringing together government and the private sector to discuss factors that constrain business development and strategies for overcoming those constraints and improving the business environment. This module considers how to ensure that the voices of women entrepreneurs are fully heard in PPD by strengthening the engagement of women in advocating for, contributing to, and playing leadership roles in reform. Reforms are more likely to benefit women when their voices are heard at the policy level—identifying critical reform areas, designing solutions, and in ensuring that reform is implemented in ways that benefit women as well as men.

This module should be read in conjunction with the Public-Private Dialogue Handbook and other guidance materials accessible at IFC's PPD Web site.[1] Bear in mind that some aspects of facilitating women's inclusion in processes of investment climate reform are beyond the framework of PPD. Consequently, not all items considered in this module will necessarily be part of PPD processes.

1

What Is PPD and Why Does Gender Matter?

PPD is increasingly regarded as an essential component of effective private sector policy reform (box 1.1). All of the topics covered in the modules of this *Practitioners' Guide* can be discussed and resolved through good public-private dialogue. It is an essential component of the diagnostic, solution design, and implementation stages of investment climate reform.

PPD is regarded as an important means of "enlarging the reform space," by ensuring greater inclusion of stakeholders in reform deliberations and facilitating greater local ownership of reform measures (figure 1.1). As this *Practitioners' Guide* shows, women in the private sector may experience different legal, regulatory, and administrative barriers to business than their male counterparts. Legal frameworks

---

BOX 1.1 **The Importance of Public-Private Dialogue in Investment Climate Reform**

Public-private dialogue plays a key role in promoting and implementing enabling environment reform. Governments that listen to the private sector are more likely to promote sensible, workable reforms. Entrepreneurs who understand what government is trying to achieve are more likely to support these reforms. Talking together is the best way for the public and private sectors to set priorities and support common interests. Meeting on a regular basis builds trust and understanding. Failure to communicate leads to failure to understand each other's concerns, which, in turn, leads to distrust and noncooperation. Noncooperation leads to inefficiency and waste, which inhibits growth, investment, and poverty reduction.

PPD is a force to counter policy making by shouting, or by back-room deals involving a select few. The loudest voices rarely speak in the best interests of private sector growth as a whole or of poverty reduction. Individual deal making inevitably leads to inconsistent and ineffective policy and regulation. By contrast, PPD promotes good public and corporate governance. It sets an example of transparency and dynamism. It sheds light on the workings and performance of government institutions. It also improves the quality of the advice government receives from the private sector by diversifying sources and by promoting more evidence-based advocacy. PPD is not a panacea, but it is an important ingredient in strong business-enabling environments. Both the public and the private sector still need good information, good analysis, and a sustained commitment to implement change.

Source: Gamser, Kadritzke, and Waddington 2005.

may deny them rights to land or property, and sociocultural factors may prevent them from engaging in business without the consent of their husbands, limit their mobility and capacity to network, or subject them to sexual or other forms of harassment from public officials. Moreover, women's presence in the private sector, as important economic actors in their own right, is not matched by their representation in policy- and decision-making institutions in the sector, including within PPD structures (box 1.2), yet there is a clear economic argument for enhanced female participation in private sector development (see introduction and economic rationale section). These factors all suggest that proactive gender inclusion can make an important contribution to improving the business environment.

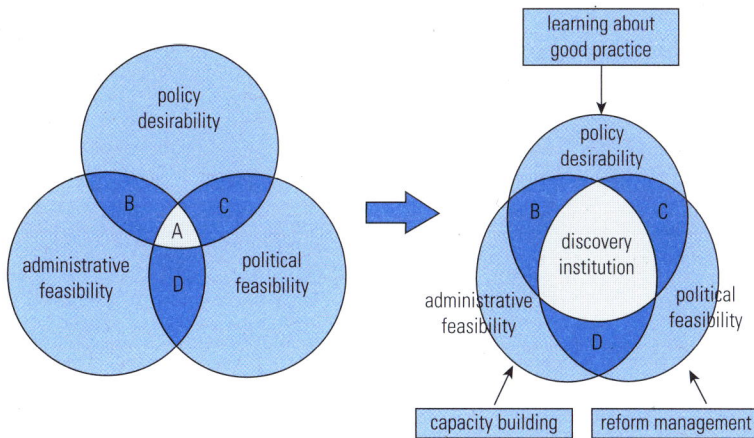

Figure 1.1   PPD—Enlarging the Reform Space

Sources: World Development Report 2005, and B. Herzberg. Powerpoint Presentation, *PPD Product Review*, IFC, November 2008.

BOX 1.2   Forms of Public-Private Dialogue

PPD often occurs within the context of a business forum, regular round-table discussion, or investment council meetings. In addition, working groups may be set up within these larger structures to deal with specific sectors or topics; for example, there may be a special group dealing with issues of concern to small businesses, export promotion, or retailers. It is important for men and women to be engaged in both national and working group discussions.

(Continued)

1

BOX 1.2 **Forms of Public-Private Dialogue (*Continued*)**

Often, outside of these formal PPD structures. informal networking links government and private sector representatives. It may be difficult at times for women to be included in this informal PPD networking because of cultural constraints, for example, if networking takes place in men's exclusive meeting places and clubs. However, women's business associations often also have a strong networking element and provide an opportunity to define issues of concern to their members that can be raised at the formal structures.

PPD can take place at all levels of the economy: between central government and private sector organizations representing national and international corporations and between local authorities and businesses. Most women entrepreneurs have small businesses operating at local market level, and therefore it is particularly important to strengthen local PPD opportunities and to ensure women are fully engaged.

Step 1 Diagnostic

Step 1 provides tools to analyze the extent to which existing or potential PPD structures are able to incorporate gender issues. These tools should be used in conjunction with the "mapping tools" for diagnosing the status and potential of PPDs contained in the PPD Handbook. The steps in the baseline diagnostic outlined in the handbook are illustrated in figure 1.2.

1.1 Consider Existing Business Organizations through a Gender Lens

Five stakeholder groups are important for the PPD process: the private sector, intermediaries, public authorities, civil society, and development partners. Two critical tasks need to be undertaken: (i) Measure gender inclusion and representativeness in all groups, especially intermediaries, if such intermediaries include women's business associations or other groups with a mandate to represent the women's business interests. (ii) During an analysis of the stakeholder groups, review the extent to which they are effectively representing these interests. Table 1.1 sets out some issues to consider in relation to gender when undertaking a standard review of existing private sector organizations as part of a PPD baseline diagnostic.

Figure 1.2 Steps in the PPD Diagnostic Process

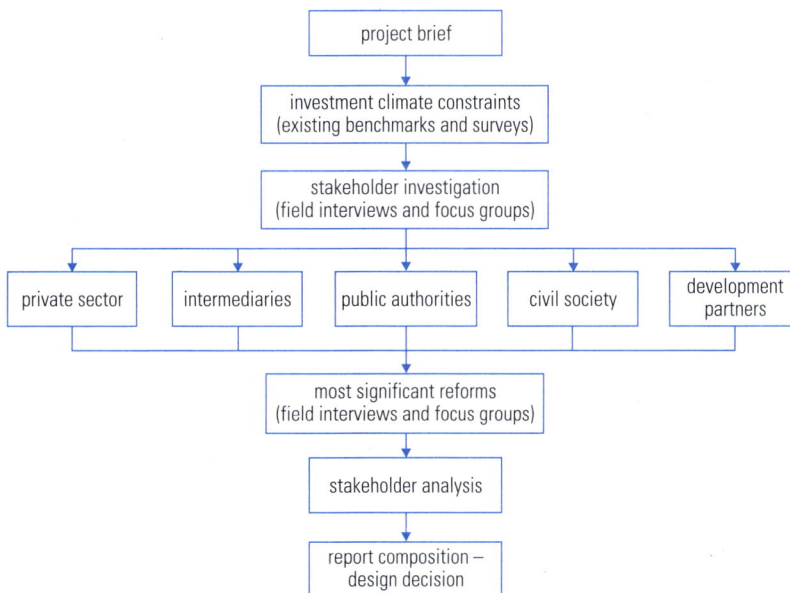

Source: PPD Handbook 2006.

1

Table 1.1: Standard Diagnostic Questions for Private Sector Organizations and Gender Dimensions

Possible standard question	Gender aspect
Do private sector representative organizations exist? What kind? What size businesses do they represent? And what type of business? (A particular sector? Region? Type of management or ownership?)	Consider whether there are separate organizations representing women in business. Consider membership of existing associations representing both men and women in business—what is the gender balance in terms of (i) membership and (ii) officials? Do women hold positions of responsibility and leadership in these organizations? Are sectors dominated by women owners represented? Are micro and small businesses represented as well as larger firms? Or is there a special section for micro and small; in which case, is this represented in discussions with government?
Are they vibrant and inclusive or moribund and captured by narrow interest groups? Which are the most effective organizations? Which have the most potential?	If women's business groups exist, what is their scope, mandate, and reach? Do they aim to represent the interests of all women in business (most of whom are likely to be informal or semi-informal)?
How effective are intermediary organizations at representing their members at national and local levels?	In the case of organizations representing both men and women in business, consider how aware the organization is of the particular issues faced by women in business and how effective it is in representing them. In the case of women's business associations, do they see advocacy as part of their mandate (or are they more focused on, for example, mutual support, networking)?
What kind of services do they offer to their members? (Training? Services on behalf of public authorities? Information on laws and regulations?)	Consider whether organizations representing both men and women provide sufficient services to their female members. Consider what services female-only business organizations provide.
What kind of information dissemination services do they provide? Do they organize regular meetings? Do they gather information on the binding constraints faced by their members?	Consider whether organizations representing both men and women provide such services aimed specifically at their female members. Consider arrangements for meetings: are these likely to be at times when women can attend, for example, midday rather than evenings? Consider what services female-only business organizations provide.

Do they have any important recent accomplishments?

What have organizations representing both men and women achieved specifically for women?
What have women's business associations achieved?

What is the importance of other kinds of intermediaries between government and the private sector, such as lawyers and notaries?

How successful are such intermediaries in representing the interests of businesswomen? If there is an active women's lawyers association, to what extent is investment climate reform part of its mandate? If it is not currently, could it be?

Are there institutional linkages between business membership organizations and government agencies or public bodies?
Are these linkages formal or informal? Regular or ad hoc?

With which parts of government are organizations representing women in business linked? Are these the more influential parts of government, such as ministry of finance, economics, planning, or trade?

Are these types of linkages with government of the same status for business organizations representing only women as they are for organizations representing both men and women? And the same status for micro and small firms, formal and informal, as for large corporations?

1

1.2 Consider Existing PPD Structures through a Gender Lens

It is important to assess how well the PPD structure responds to gender concerns. If there is an existing mechanism for public-private dialogue (for example, a business roundtable or investor council), consider the extent to which the interests of women are adequately represented in this forum. While the precise form of a PPD may vary (box 1.3), the core questions to ask with respect to gender in the structure are summarized below.

BOX 1.3 Typical Structure of a PPD

There is no one-size-fits-all structure to successful PPD. In fact, institutional design depends on a number of variables, and identifying the variables and the options for adapting to them properly. There may be different organizational forms depending on the degree of organization of the private sector, the power of the executive versus the legislature, the structure of the private sector and of the government.

A setting that seems to be prevalent in the most productive PPDs is characterized by a dedicated secretariat and working groups that meet often to devise recommendations for periodic plenary sessions.

The function of the secretariat is to organize meetings, coordinate research efforts and other logistics, set agendas, rally members, manage communication and outreach strategies, and be a point of contact for others who want to join.

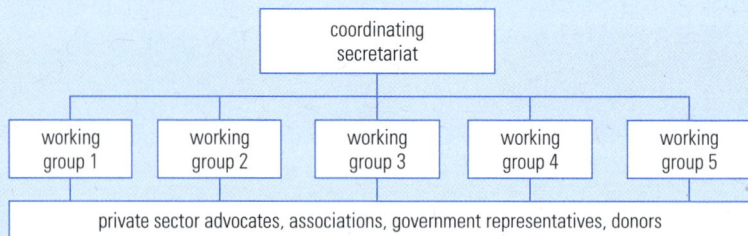

```
                    ┌──────────────────┐
                    │   coordinating   │
                    │   secretariat    │
                    └──────────────────┘
     ┌──────────┬──────────┼──────────┬──────────┐
┌─────────┐┌─────────┐┌─────────┐┌─────────┐┌─────────┐
│ working ││ working ││ working ││ working ││ working │
│ group 1 ││ group 2 ││ group 3 ││ group 4 ││ group 5 │
└─────────┘└─────────┘└─────────┘└─────────┘└─────────┘
┌─────────────────────────────────────────────────────┐
│ private sector advocates, associations, government   │
│ representatives, donors                              │
└─────────────────────────────────────────────────────┘
```

Working groups are typically organized by one or more of the following criteria: industry cluster (for example, agriculture, tourism, or manufacturing), by policy issue (for example, deregulation, infrastructure, or labor) or by geographical location. This enables them to focus more effectively and call on greater levels of technical expertise.

Working groups meet more frequently than plenary groups. They typically have a chair who deals with other working groups and the secretariat, by which they are coordinated and supervised. They feed policy recommendations into plenary sessions.

Source: PPD Handbook 2006.

1

Gender PPD Checklist of Key Questions

- How many members of the PPD forum have the specific mandate to represent the interests of businesswomen?
- What linkages do members of the PPD forum have with businesswomen or with women's business organizations?
- What activities has the PPD forum undertaken to identify and act on the specific barriers faced by women in business?
- What business-enabling environment issues that affect women has the forum discussed in the past six months (or year)?
- Are there success stories of tackling investment issues that had an impact on women?

1.3 If Appropriate, Undertake Preliminary Dialogue with Businesswomen

It is important to build on existing initiatives and dialogue processes where possible. But where these do not exist, are weak, or do not represent the interests of businesswomen, it may be useful to initiate new forums for businesswomen, to strengthen existing forums, or simply to provide a mechanism to facilitate consultation between women in business and other stakeholders. Care should be taken to ensure the process includes very small businesses that may not be organized into formal associations (box 1.4).

BOX 1.4 **Dialogue with Women in Business (See also Core Module)**

During an IFC diagnostic mission in the **South Pacific** to review the scope for incorporation of gender into IFC's investment climate reform initiatives, IFC initiated women's business forums in Papua New Guinea, Samoa, the Solomon Islands, and Tonga. Where possible, forums were organized using the offices of existing women's business organizations (for example, the Solomon Islands Women in Business Association). But in Papua New Guinea, where the women's business association was weak and fairly unrepresentative, invitations were sent to businesswomen through a variety of means. In Tonga, the forum was organized by the advisory team implementing the regulatory simplification project, whereas in Samoa the forum was organized through the dynamic leadership of the Small Business Enterprise Centre.

(Continued)

1

> ### BOX 1.4 Dialogue with Women in Business (See also Core Module) (*Continued*)
>
> Forums were informal, with the clear objective for the women to share stories of the constraints they face related to the investment climate and with a view to influencing IFC programs to address women's concerns. In the Solomon Islands and Papua New Guinea, as an icebreaker, women were asked to share in pairs what they "loved" about being in business and what they "hated"—and answers were pinned to the walls for sharing. Networking and relationships came out as key positives. In breakout groups, women who had encountered problems in particular areas (for example, business start-up or dispute resolution) were asked to provide details, using the questionnaires in this *Practitioners' Guide*. The session ended with a prioritization exercise, with participants voting on which solutions to problems encountered were the most important to take forward.
>
> Feedback from the forums indicated that the women appreciated the chance to network and share common concerns: many business cards were exchanged. In Papua New Guinea, it is hoped that the forum can develop into an ongoing mechanism for businesswomen and feed into new structures being developed for PPD. In the Solomon Islands, the forum was an opportunity to strengthen the existing Women in Business Association and to encourage new members to join. In Samoa, the forum was seen as a useful starting point for strengthening women's engagement in existing mechanisms of dialogue with the government, and, possibly, helping to establish the foundations for a future public-private dialogue initiative.
>
> *Source:* Based on authors' field research.

Step 2   Solution Design

The diagnostic step may reveal that there is scope for strengthening organizations and structures to ensure that women's voices are adequately represented in PPD and that there is effective advocacy on investment climate reform issues that affect women. Step 2 presents potential solutions to address these issues. These are not "one-size-fits-all" solutions, but rather examples of approaches that will need to be adapted for particular contexts. Although PPD programs supported by IFC do not usually engage in building the capacity of the participating organizations and structures, capacity building may be required to integrate gender concerns effectively into PPD processes. This guide provides suggestions for how capacity-building efforts can be supported in the framework of PPD, even where this support may be provided by other partners.

2.1   Ensure Women Are Represented in Public-Private Dialogue Structures

Public-private dialogue structures (for example, business roundtables or investor councils) should include people or organizations able to represent the concerns of women as well as men. The Beijing Platform for Action target for women's representation on public bodies to be at least 30 percent may be a starting point. However, the women on the body must represent the range of women's business interests across business size and sector and must address substantive investment climate issues as well as where these affect women differently than men.

As discussed in relation to monitoring and evaluation (see core module), women entrepreneurs are often not well represented in membership-based private sector associations. There may be several reasons for this: Women may have been excluded; they may have less time to participate in activities beyond their business and domestic responsibilities; they may be unwelcome or not feel "comfortable" at meetings attended mainly by men; they may have mobility or other constraints; or the associations may represent interests outside their business sector. If the diagnostic reveals that women are not adequately represented in business associations and that this results in underrepresentation in PPD structures, possible solutions are

- to encourage existing private sector organizations to broaden their membership base to include more women and, at the same time, encourage more women to get involved in these;
- to work with businesswomen and encourage them to set up women's business associations to engage in PPD; and
- to include in PPD mechanisms organizations not normally involved in such structures, but having experience and knowledge of the issues facing women

1

in business. This may include nongovernmental organizations (NGOs), microfinance institutions (who will have many businesswomen as their clients), and projects focusing on improving livelihoods at the community level or other grassroots organizations.

Clearly, gender inclusion in PPD processes sometimes requires proactive outreach and effort (box 1.5). Representation of women's interests in PPD structures should include both private sector organizations as well as any governmental bodies responsible for taking forward gender policies (for example, the ministry for women, gender/equality commission, national council for women, or gender focal points within other government ministries).

2.2 Undertake Training and Capacity-Building Activities and Build Coalitions

Many countries have mature women's groups advocating for gender equality and improved women's rights. But such groups may have limited skills or knowledge in relation to technical investment climate issues. In Uganda, some success was achieved in relation to legal and regulatory reform aimed at benefiting women (box 1.6). In this case, legal skills on commercial laws were necessary for effective Gender and Growth Assessment (GGA) coalition participation in the policy debate. Effective advocates in the realm of gender issues thus may require capacity building to extend their skills to investment climate issues. Conversely, organizations representing business interests to government may require capacity building in relation to gender issues.

Partnerships and dialogue among organizations with technical gender expertise, particularly in advocacy and those with private sector development or investment climate reform expertise, may be fruitful in taking effective advocacy forward.

BOX 1.5 **Involve Women and Minority Groups**

Organizers must reach out to women and minority groups if they do not come forward. Their proportional participation creates balance, sets an example, and helps create a more favorable public image. Favoring companies with a good record of corporate social responsibility and corporate governance also sets a good example.

Source: PPD Handbook 2006.

1

BOX 1.6 **Uganda: Gender Coalition—Building Capacity to Lobby for Change**

Uganda's Ministry for Finance requested IFC to assess the country's investment climate through a gender lens. The resulting analysis and recommendations were published in Uganda's Gender and Growth Assessment.[2] An IFC GGA team followed up with a two-day workshop on advocacy and public-private dialogue. During the workshop a GGA coalition with representatives of seven women's organizations was formed to take the recommendations forward through lobbying and advocacy. The coalition's members focused on thematic areas of the GGA according to their technical areas of expertise. Legal and regulatory reform is a complex and time-consuming process and impacts may be observed over several years, but some positive results have already emerged:

- GGA recommendations have been incorporated into Uganda's Private Sector Development Strategy 2005–2009 (UP3) and the National Gender Strategy 2005–2014.
- Labor laws were reformed through the Employment Bill, the Occupational Safety and Health Bill, the Labor Dispute Bill, and the Labor Unions Bill, which were passed in March 2006 and are awaiting the assent of the president. Following lobbying from the GGA coalition, GGA recommendations were incorporated into the four bills.

Source: Ellis et al. 2006.

2.3 Adopt Proactive Policies to Strengthen Women's Voices

If the political climate is right, it may be possible to take high-level action to entrench businesswomen's voices in government policy. Improved data collection and a robust organization tasked to provide advice to government on women's entrepreneurship may be achieved by administrative action, rather than legislation. The U.S. experience demonstrates the impact that a high-level mandate for strengthening the voices of women entrepreneurs can have (box 1.7).

Other ways of promoting gender-informed investment climate reform, beyond the specific mechanism of PPD, include strategic communication and strengthening the role of local champions. These two elements were combined by IFC when it launched an information campaign to raise awareness of women's role in business in Indonesia. The campaign recognized that improving the business environment for women would demand more than reform, but a "changed mind-set" (box 1.8).

1

BOX 1.7   Promoting Women in Business in the United States

The **United States** 1988 Women's Business Ownership Act[3] addresses the needs of women in business through such actions as the establishment of Women's Business Center "demonstration sites." In addition, the act enhanced businesswomen's ability to advocate effectively in two important ways:

- It strengthened data collection about female-headed businesses, requiring agencies involved in implementing the act to ensure systematic data collection about women in business, and strengthened the U.S. Census Bureau's reporting on women's businesses.
- It created the National Women's Business Council, consisting of women entrepreneurs and women's organizations, to advise the president, Congress, and the Small Business Association on policy and program recommendations.

The act is credited with contributing to the growth in the number of female-owned enterprises in the United States by 20 percent between 1997 and 2002, twice the national average for all businesses, generating more than $940 billion in revenue.

Source: U.S. Census Bureau 2006.

BOX 1.8   Stakeholder Engagement in Indonesia

Although women in **Indonesia** owned 60 percent of the country's formal and informal micro, small- and medium-scale enterprises (SMEs), they were often denied credit without approval from a husband. This was one of many paradoxes on which IFC sought to shed light through a public outreach campaign aimed at increasing awareness of women's role in business. Two stakeholders, the State Ministry of Women Empowerment and the Indonesian Women's Business Association, were critical to the campaign and to future reform efforts. The project team dedicated six months to presenting its research findings and building consensus with the two stakeholders on messages, facts, figures, and issues to be communicated. The team sought to tap into a deep understanding of existing perceptions, as well as local support, for the endeavor in order to understand the sociocultural environment, draw on the experiences of local stakeholders to gather input, develop strategies to ensure that the issue would be addressed effectively, ensure messages would resonate among target audiences, and

(Continued)

1

| BOX 1.8 | **Stakeholder Engagement in Indonesia (*Continued*)** |

unleash women's economic potential. The campaign drew on two research publications with overtly different approaches:

- *Access to Credit for Businesswomen in Indonesia* showcased analytical findings to be leveraged in policy discussions or distilled for general audiences.
- *Voices of Women in the Private Sector* presented stories of women entrepreneurs that a wider audience could understand and with which they could empathize.

Both approaches were important to the project's dual goals of encouraging policy responsiveness and raising public awareness. Survey findings can be used by the policy community that will eventually be critical to supporting and pushing through the reforms to improve the business climate for women. Communicating similar information through anecdotes and individual stories will more likely gain the interest of a broader audience base.

Source: Adapted from World Bank 2007.

2.4 Link Advocacy to CEDAW and Other International Reporting Processes

CEDAW obligates signatory countries to ensure that women have the same opportunities as men to participate in economic life and to remove legal and regulatory barriers that discriminate against women (see annex A of the core module). Signatory countries are obliged to submit periodic[4] reports to the CEDAW Committee at the United Nations on their progress toward meeting their CEDAW commitments. NGOs are encouraged to participate in the process of monitoring a country's compliance with CEDAW by submitting a "shadow" CEDAW report[5] critiquing the "official" report. In Bosnia, in the absence of an official report, NGOs produced a shadow report,[6] which, in turn, prompted the government to comply with its reporting obligations.[7]

It is frequently NGOs, rather than private sector associations, that take the lead in advocacy around CEDAW and in putting pressure on government to comply with its CEDAW obligations. CEDAW reporting is an internationally recognized and respected mechanism and an effective advocacy tool to advance legal, regulatory, and administrative reforms to benefit women in business at the country level. It may therefore be appropriate to make linkages between PPD mechanisms (which typically involve business associations and government agencies responsible for private sector development) and CEDAW reporting mechanisms (which typically involve

1

NGOs and government agencies responsible for women's affairs). The appropriate way to make the linkage between public-private dialogue processes and the CEDAW reporting process will vary from country to country. Possible entry points may be

- to have CEDAW compliance and reporting on the agenda of the PPD forum;
- if there is an ongoing CEDAW reporting process, for business organizations to use it as an advocacy platform with government; and
- if NGOs are producing a shadow CEDAW report, for business organizations to engage with NGOs and participate in developing the section on economic empowerment.

The five yearly reports on the indicators agreed upon for the Beijing Platform for Action constitute another international reporting process that can provide an opportunity to ensure women's business needs are being addressed on the same level as men's.

2.5   Draw on International Resources

There are a number of international resources that can provide support with country-level advocacy. Some of these initiatives are outlined in box 1.9.

In addition, inspiration may be obtained from international experience of successful advocacy to support women's businesses (box 1.10). Where appropriate, it may be possible to organize study tours to learn from such experience and to form partnerships with successful groups.

> **BOX 1.9**   **Other Resources for Country-Level Advocacy**
>
> The **ILO's WEDGE program** promotes the "Month of the Woman Entrepreneur" in African countries (to date, **Ethiopia, Tanzania, Uganda,** and **Zambia**). This is a series of events designed to promote awareness about women's entrepreneurship, encourage sharing of experiences, and to inspire the design of future strategies to assist women entrepreneurs and strengthen the capacities of their associations. The media are central to these events. In both Tanzania and Uganda, workshops were held on the role of the media in women's entrepreneurship development. The media were also actively involved in the events themselves. In Tanzania, newspaper, radio, and television journalists attended the launch of the month's events, and a "Road Show" toured Dar es Salaam.
>
> *(Continued)*

1

BOX 1.9   Other Resources for Country-Level Advocacy (*Continued*)

The Community of Women Entrepreneurs, a Web site hosted and moderated by the U.S. Center for International Private Enterprise, is a forum for sharing ideas, experiences, best practices, and resources to empower women economically and politically. Members of this community are leading entrepreneurs and business advocates who share their knowledge and in return receive fresh ideas from their peers. Discussion in this community focuses on supporting a culture of entrepreneurship, expanding the opportunities for women in business, and advocating for a better business environment.

BOX 1.10   Successful Advocacy Efforts

In the **United Kingdom**, PROWESS is an association of more than 300 organizations and individuals who support the growth of women's business ownership. Their activities include lobbying and advocacy at national, regional, European, and local levels. For example, at its annual conference in March 2009, PROWESS rallied the U.K. business support network for urgent action to ensure women business owners can lead the way out of the recession. Top of its list was a call on the government to remove the blockage that is being caused by the banks preventing renewals of and extensions to overdrafts and loans. PROWESS is also lobbying for the government to design programs of support, such as that given to the car industry, to better respond to female dimensions of the recession. In 2003 PROWESS collaborated with the government's Small Business Service to develop a Strategic Framework for Women's Enterprise ("Sharing the Vision: a collaborative approach to increasing female entrepreneurship").[8] This commits the government to support and encourage the development of strategic partnerships and implementation of change in policy and practice.

In **Romania,** the Coalition of Women Business Associations (CAFA) was created in 2004 when nine local women's business associations joined together to create one voice for women entrepreneurs to participate in public policy and provide input on economic policy in Romania. Since its formation, CAFA has participated in many public policy debates and organized itself as an informal coalition with a communication center. In April 2009, CAFA members will meet in Timisoara, in the western part of Romania, where one important topic on its agenda is to prepare a position paper on fighting recent government attempts to increase taxes. For CAFA this

(*Continued*)

1

BOX 1.10 **Successful Advocacy Efforts (*Continued*)**

meeting is not only about sharing experience, it is also about building a common voice to support the interests of Romanian women entrepreneurs.

In **Nepal,** the Federation of Woman Entrepreneurs Associations of Nepal advocates for policies and programs concerning women's issues for national socioeconomic development.

Source: For example from United Kingdom, see PROWESS, from Romania, see CAFA and from Nepal, see Currier and Rotaru 2009.

Step 3   Implementation and M&E

The baseline elements on monitoring and evaluation in the core module should be applied to PPD programs. PPD programs have developed an extensive M&E system, which is outlined in the PPD Handbook. The suggestions for gender-focused M&E made here should be examined in conjunction with the M&E framework in the PPD Handbook.

A key element of the PPD M&E framework is the evaluation wheel, which facilitates assessment of the core elements of a PPD program (figure 1.3). These elements are summarized in the annex A to this module, along with questions addressing the gender dimensions of the core elements.

In addition, the following points should be considered in relation to M&E.

3.1   Incorporate Indicators That Highlight Gender Aspects of Public-Private Dialogue

Table 1.2 provides a template for incorporating gender in the core **investment climate** (IC) indicators typically used to measure the progress of public-private dialogue.

An important dimension of monitoring and evaluation is assessement of the process so as to gain a better idea of the impact of public-private dialogue on the

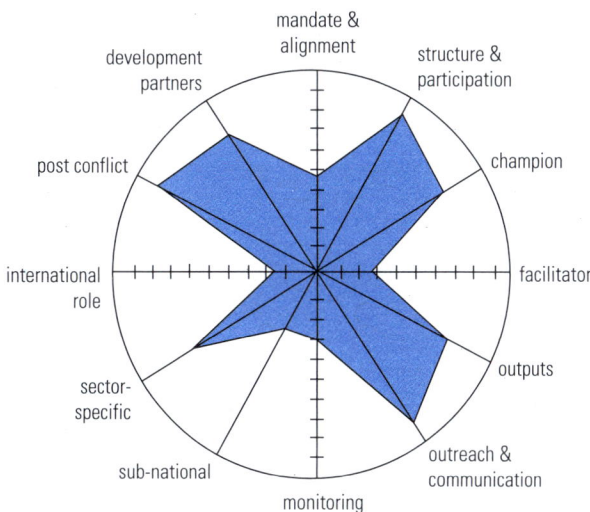

Figure 1.3   Sample Evaluation Wheel for PPD

Source: PPD Handbook 2006.

1

Table 1.2: M&E Indicators

Indicator/Data required	Gender focus (Gender disaggregation)	Source of data
Output indicators		

• Representation in PPD institutions:
  • Task force
  • Working groups
  • Secretariat
	• Number and/or percentage of men and women (men's and women's businesses) represented in these institutions
	• Percentage of men and women managers and staff in the PPD secretariat
		• PPD secretariat
		• Meeting minutes and reports

• Number of meetings of PPD task force and working groups	• Number and/or percentage of men and women at these meetings	• Meeting minutes and reports
• Substantive PPD and reform issues discussed	• Qualitative indicator: extent of attention to gender issues in the substantive agenda	• PPD secretariat • Meeting minutes and reports
• PPD institutions: operation and accessibility	• Timing of meetings suitable for women • Accessible and safe location • Welcoming of women	• Focus group discussions (FGDs) • PPD secretariat • Women's business associations
• Number of operational manuals produced • Training and outreach	• Qualitative indicator: gender-inclusive focus; gender issues articulated and addressed • Core indicator: number and/or percentage of men and women participating or benefiting	• Manuals produced • PPD secretariat • FGDs • Interviews with businesswomen
• Number of media appearances and other outreach and communications	• Number and/or percentage of men and women at these appearances • Attention to gender issues in media appearances	• Media reports
Outcome indicators		
PPD reforms implemented	• Gender-responsiveness of reforms implemented • Proactive engagement of women (and women's associations) in reform programs	• PPD secretariat • FGDs • Women's businesses and associations

reforms undertaken. This involves determining key steps in the reform process, that is, drafting, adopting, and implementing legal or regulatory reforms. In the matrix in figure 1.4, the columns represent the specific steps of the process, and the rows represent specific reform measures included in the PPD. The evaluator rates the steps according to the extent to which the PPD process influenced the step, ranging from 0 (no influence) to 3 (PPD solely responsible for the step). To the extent that the issue is of particular relevance to businesswomen, the influence of the PPD on the steps taken to move the issue forward can be assessed in a manner complementary to the formal M&E of outputs, outcomes, and impacts.

Figure 1.4 PPD Process Evaluation: Cambodia

issue	1.0	2.0	3.0	4.0	5.0	6.0	7.0	8.0	9.0	10.0	11.0	12.0	13.0	average
1.0	-	-	1.0	2.0	1.0	2.0	2.0	3.0			2.0	2.0	1.0	1.5
2.0	-		1.0	1.0	1.0				-	-	-	2.0	-	0.5
3.0	-		1.0	2.0	2.0	2.0	1.0	3.0	1.0	2.0			1.0	1.4
4.0	-	1.0	1.0	1.0	1.0	2.0	1.0	2.0	2.0	-		1.0	-	0.9
5.0	-	1.0	1.0	2.0	2.0	3.0	2.0	2.0	-	1.0	-	2.0	-	1.2
6.0	-	-	-	2.0	1.0	2.0		3.0	-	2.0	-	3.0	-	1.1
average	-	0.3	0.8	1.7	1.3	2.2	1.5	2.6	0.6	1.0	0.4	2.0	0.3	1.1

Source: Herzberg 2009.

Annex A   PPD Evaluation Wheel

Adapting the Questionnaire to Stakeholders to Address Gender-Related Issues

Please give your personal opinion on each question, expressing your answer on a scale of 0 to 5 (with "0" being "worst" and "5" being "best"). If you are not well informed enough to offer an opinion, please score 0.

#	Subquestion	Gender focus
	Mandate and institutional alignment—What were or are the objectives of the PPD, and what was or is its mandate toward the government and the private sector? How does it fit with current institutions?	
1	Existence of mission statement and capacity of participants to explain this mission statement	Does the mission statement explicitly address gender equality and/or women's issues?
2	Degree of anchorage of the partnership in existing public institutions as per its mandate	Does a gender focus contribute to recognition of the PPD and to the attitude toward your partnership?
3	Institutional readiness to implement PPD recommendations	What is the respective contribution of men and women to PPD institutional readiness?
	Structure and participation—How is the PPD structured; does it enable a balanced and effective participation?	
4	Existence of rules and regulations in the partnership, including formal mechanisms in place to balance power	Are women equally represented in PPD structures and possibilities to participate in the partnership?
5	Degree of participatory decision making	Do women participate in PPD decision making?
	Champion(s) and leadership—Has the PPD identified champions, and how has it tried to leverage them over time to impact the effectiveness of the dialogue process?	
6	The presence and clear involvement of champions who are recognized as such by stakeholders	Are there female champions? Do the champions represent women's issues?
7	Continuity of involvement of champions in dialogue or in partnership	Is there continuity in women's leadership and presence in the PPD?
	Facilitation and management—Did the PPD engage suitable facilitators and/or managers? How has their role been defined? Have they managed to effectively ensure cohesion and performance? What conflicts did they manage, and how did they resolve these?	
8	Quality of facilitation of the PPD	Are there women facilitators? Do they address women's issues?
9	Quality of PPD logistics and management arrangements (responsibilities, tasks, structure, logistics, and so on)	Are women adequately represented in PPD management?

(Continued)

1

#	Subquestion	Gender focus

Outputs—What outputs does the PPD produce, and under what internal processes? Have outputs from the PPD contributed to agreed-on private sector development outcomes in the shape of structure and process outputs, analytical outputs, or recommendations?

#	Subquestion	Gender focus
10	Hard outputs: analytical reports, reviews, and so on	Do the hard outputs of the PPD address gender issues?
11	Soft outputs: respondents reporting improved trust, cooperation, communication, and so on	What are the shares of men and women reporting improved trust, cooperation, communication, and so on?
12	Impact output: Degree to which dialogue or partnership has innovated or changed existing institutional structures	Has the PPD been able to influence changes that are gender responsive?

Outreach and communication—Has the PPD communication enabled a shared vision and understanding through the development of a common language and built trust among stakeholders?

#	Subquestion	Gender focus
13	Quality and frequency of communication among different stakeholder groups	Is the PPD communication gender inclusive?
14	Amount and kind of outreach and communication activities to civil society and media	Is there outreach and awareness-raising specifically focused on women's issues or groups?

Monitoring—Is there regular reporting on the process, activities, outputs, and outcomes of the PPD, and provision of follow-up actions to problems identified in these reports?

#	Subquestion	Gender focus
15	Quality of reporting and documentation on activities of the partnership	Are gender-focused outputs and outcomes monitored?
16	Degree to which monitoring results have resulted in changes in planning and targets	Has gender-focused monitoring facilitated better gender-informed planning and target setting?
17	Use of ex post assessment	Has this assessment addressed the gender-responsiveness of the PPD?

Subnational—Has the dialogue been conducted at all levels of decision making down to the most local level possible and involving microentrepreneurs, SMEs, and local stakeholders?

#	Subquestion	Gender focus
18	Existence of local and regional structures or consultation mechanisms for the dialogue or partnership	Does the PPD consult equally with women stakeholders?
19	Existence of activities of the PPD at other levels (local, regional, or national) through ad hoc activities, dedicated programs, or working groups	Does outreach at different levels reach women stakeholders?

(Continued)

1

#	Subquestion	Gender focus
	Sector Specific—Have sector-specific or issue-specific public-private dialogues been encouraged?	
20	Degree to which the dialogue or partnership addresses specific problems of participants	Are gender-specific sectoral issues or gender issues faced by participants addressed?
21	Capacity of the dialogue or partnership to generate concrete solutions to specific problems of participants	Does the PPD have the capacity to generate gender-responsive sector solutions?
	International role—Does the PPD represent and promote national and regional interests of both public and private actors in international negotiations and international dialogue processes?	
22	Presence and participation of participants in the dialogue or partnership at international forums and conferences	Is there gender balance in the opportunities to participate in international forums?
23	Active consultation and contacts made by international actors to learn from the dialogue or partnerships	Is gender-focused information on activities shared internationally?
	Postconflict/crisis recovery/reconciliation—Has the PPD contributed to consolidate peace and rebuild the economy through private sector development in postconflict and crisis environments, including post–natural disaster?	
24	Capacity to put conflicts on the agenda of the dialogue or partnership and resolve them	Does the PPD recognize and address gender dimensions of conflict?
25	Contributions made by the dialogue or partnership to conflict resolution and peace building in its external environment	Is the role of women in conflict resolution recognized and supported?
	Development partners—How dependent is the PPD on the input and support of donors? How has the donor agenda affected the decisions of the PPD?	
26	Degree of dependence of the PPD on financial support of development partners (DPs)	Are DPs proactive or otherwise engaged in promoting a gender focus as part of their support to the PPD?
27	Degree of autonomy of the agenda of the PPD from agendas of development partners	Do development partners influence (positively or negatively) the focus of the PPD on gender issues?
28	Degree to which the DPs give the needed assistance to the PPD facilitator	Do DPs support gender-inclusive facilitation and/or capacity building of facilitators to address gender issues?

Source: Adapted from annex D5 of the PPD Handbook, as revised in April 2009.

Notes

1. For more on PPD, see http://www.publicprivatedialogue.org/.

2. A. Ellis et al., *Gender and Economic Growth in Uganda, Directions in Development* (World Bank, 2006).

3. About.com: Women in Business. http://womeninbusiness.about.com/od/billsand laws/a/hr5050-wbo-act-htm (Accessed on September 2, 2009).

4. The first report should be submitted within one year of ratification and subsequent reports every four years thereafter.

5. To learn more about how NGOs can submit a "shadow" CEDAW report, see http://www.un.org/womenwatch/daw/cedaw/NGO_Information_note_CEDAW.pdf

6. However, shadow reports may not be submitted to the committee in the absence of an official report.

7. See http://www.globalrights.org/site/MessageViewer?em_id=5101.0

8. PROWESS, http://www.prowess.org.uk/publications.htm

1

Business Entry and Operations: Registration, Licensing, and Permits

This Module Should be Used in Conjunction with the Core Module

This module (i) suggests tools to explore gender differences in business entry and operation (step 1 – diagnostics); (ii) provides possible solutions to address gender-related constraints identified (step 2 – solution design); and (iii) suggests ways to incorporate gender considerations into implementation and monitoring and evaluation of business entry and operation programs (step 3 – implementation and monitoring and evaluation).

Summary

MODULE 2

Why Gender Matters

This module considers the impact of gender on the processes necessary to start and operate a business on a formal basis—registration, licensing, and permits.[1] There is growing evidence that women can find it more difficult than men to formalize their businesses. Legal or cultural limitations on their ability to travel may mean that women cannot get to a registry to lodge the necessary documents; time poverty (a result of dual business and domestic responsibilities) may also constrain women's ability to undertake the bureaucratic steps necessary to formalize the businesses; lower educational and business skills training levels may mean that women are less aware than men of the formalization process; and often when women seek to interact with bureaucratic procedures, they are much more likely than men to suffer harassment (including sexual harassment) and be disadvantaged in their dealings with public officials.

> *"Most of our policies and legislation were meant for big business, not for small businesses where women are."*
>
> – Focus group discussion with women entrepreneurs, Tanzania

Worldwide, women are three times more likely than men to be found in the informal economy.[2] Typically women owners represent a minority of registered businesses, for example, less than 10 percent in the Democratic Republic of Congo and about 40 percent in Rwanda[3] (see figure 2.1. with evidence from Africa).

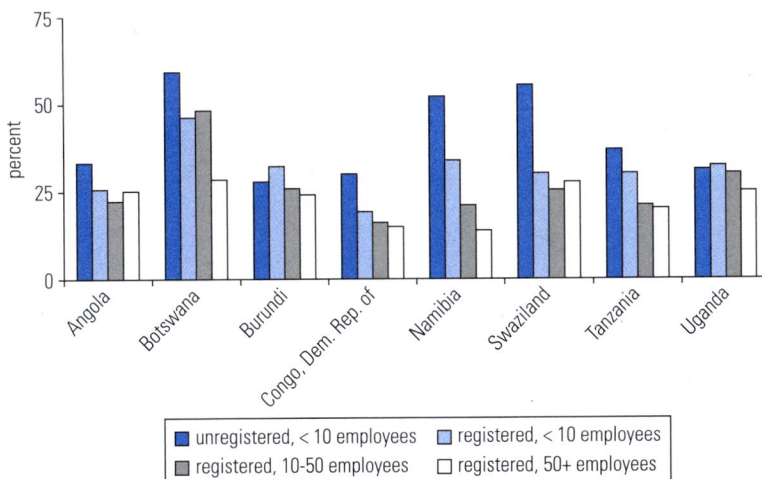

Figure 2.1   Female Entrepreneurs in the Informal Sector

Legend:
- unregistered, < 10 employees
- registered, < 10 employees
- registered, 10-50 employees
- registered, 50+ employees

Countries: Angola, Botswana, Burundi, Congo, Dem. Rep. of, Namibia, Swaziland, Tanzania, Uganda

Source: World Bank 2005.

As well as barriers presented by the formalization process, there may be other, more fundamental disincentives that cause women, more than men, to keep their businesses in the informal sector. Intrahousehold resource allocation may mean that a woman will not see the benefit of any additional income that business growth and formalization could bring, and so the incentive to formalize is low. Or the prevailing culture may restrict the women's sphere to low-level economic activity and the domestic environment (this broader social and cultural context is considered in the core module). It is unlikely that these issues can be directly tackled within the context of a regulatory reform program, but the program should be designed and implemented cognizant of them. This module provides tools to ensure that reforms put in place to ease the process of business formalization do not inadvertently discriminate against women and that they provide a framework that enables women to benefit from the regulatory reforms on the same basis as their male counterparts.

2

Step 1   Diagnostics

Step 1 provides tools to explore the legal and regulatory barriers faced by women when they (i) seek to formalize their businesses and (ii) to identify specific problems encountered by women entrepreneurs in the process. Business formalization processes may operate at national or subnational levels. For example, business licensing to a large extent is typically undertaken by local government. It may therefore be necessary to apply this module to institutions and laws at both the national and subnational level.

2

> The critical steps to be taken during an initial project design phase (in the absence of a full diagnostic at that point) are identified by a magnifying glass icon. 🔍

1.1   Assess Extent to Which Women's Businesses Are Formalized

International evidence suggests that women's businesses are more likely than men's to be operated on an informal or semi-informal basis. Analysis is needed to gain an understanding of the extent to which women's businesses are formalized. Gender-disaggregated survey evidence (for example, informality surveys or enterprise surveys) might highlight this issue. However, informal businesses, by their nature, tend to be "under the radar," and there may be limited data available. Discussions with business organizations and with government officials can provide anecdotal evidence about the extent to which formal businesses are owned or managed by women. In addition, it may be possible to conduct a "quick and dirty" analysis by considering a sample of registrations in the business registry (box 2.1).

BOX 2.1   Evidence from West Africa and the South Pacific

In recent analysis for the World Bank Group, sample data from the business registries of **Ghana, Papua New Guinea,** and the **Solomon Islands** were considered. Registrations over a two-week period from the business names registry and the companies registry were analyzed. The number of business names registrations made by (i) women, (ii) men, and (iii) in joint male-female names were counted. Similarly, in relation to companies, the number of male and female shareholders and male and female directors were counted.

In all cases, a tiny minority of registrations involved women; a large majority were to male business owners, shareholders, and directors.

Source: Authors' research.

1.2 Obtain Gender-Disaggregated Private Sector Views on Formalization

a) Use existing private sector surveys for gender-disaggregated data

Existing private sector surveys (for example, World Bank Enterprise Surveys or Administrative and Regulatory Cost Surveys) may contain gender-disaggregated data on business formalization. They may contain useful information on disparities between male and female formalization levels and perceptions of male and women entrepreneurs on obstacles to formalizing their businesses. If the published version of a relevant survey does not contain gender-disaggregated data, it may be possible to request that survey organization undertake additional analysis of the raw data to produce gender-disaggregated responses to specified survey questions. National and international nongovernmental organizations (NGOs), particularly those with a focus on gender (which may not traditionally be consulted in investment climate work), should also be requested to provide any relevant survey evidence they may have.

b) Collect New Data from the Private Sector on Formalization

Existing survey evidence on gender disparities in business formalization will likely need to be supplemented with more in-depth exploration of the nature of the disparities and the reasons for them. Key sources of information are likely to be

(i) business owners (male and female) in the informal sector—that is, who have not formalized their businesses (box 2.2);

(ii) business owners (male and female) who have formalized their businesses (or the person who actually undertook the registration or licensing process on their behalf)—especially those who have recently undertaken the process; and

(iii) business intermediaries (for example, lawyers and accountants) who undertake business registration and licensing for clients. When identifying business intermediaries, it would be helpful to include those with a background in gender

---

BOX 2.2   How to Engage with Informal Businesses

- Microfinance institutions may assist with contacts with their clients.
- NGOs working with informal sector operators may be able to provide contacts.
- Informal sector associations (for example, in Kenya, Jua Kali [Street Trader] Association) may assist.
- Direct contacts with market traders, street traders, and so forth may be possible.

2

issues. In-country women's lawyers' organizations (for example, Federacion Internacional de Abogadas [FIDA][4]) may be able to assist with identifying relevant candidates.

This is an opportunity to explore the issues relevant in sectors that have a higher share of female-run businesses (See box 2.3).

Methods for collecting new data include (i) one-on-one interviews, (ii) focus group discussions, and (iii) formal surveys.[5] Annex A contains a pro forma questionnaire that can be used as the basis for developing these tools. The questionnaire is designed to map out gender differences in the processes, as well as explore the reasons for men's and women's choices on whether to formalize their businesses.

2

1.3 Develop Inventory of the Licensing and Permit Framework

The requirement for registration applies to all relevant businesses, but the licensing and permitting regime varies by business sector. As discussed in the core module, differences frequently exist between the types of businesses men and women operate—in size, place in the value chain, and economic sector. For this reason, it is important to ensure that the licensing or permit regime is mapped as fully as possible[6] and an analysis undertaken of which licenses are most relevant to businesses in which women predominate and which apply to male-dominated sectors or types of businesses.

BOX 2.3 **Definition of "Female-Headed Businesses"**

When collecting data, it is important to be clear about distinctions between female "-owned," "-managed," or "-headed" businesses. Most businesses in the informal sector are owned and managed by the same person. But this is not always the case. For example, in Kampala, **Uganda,** "boda boda" (motorbike taxi) operators are almost exclusively men. However, the male operators are increasingly working for female bike owners.

The U.S. Women's Business Ownership Act provides a helpful definition of a "woman-owned business" as one that is at least 51 percent owned by a woman or women who also control and operate it. "Control" in this context means exercising the power to make policy decisions. "Operate" in this context means being actively involved in the day-to-day management. "Woman's business enterprise" is defined as a woman-owned business or businesses or the efforts of a woman or women to establish, maintain, or develop such a business or businesses.

Source: U.S. Women's Business Ownership Act of 1988 and Executive Order 12138.

1.4 Document Detailed Registration, Licensing, and Permit Processes through a Gender Lens

The basis for regulatory simplification is an understanding of how each process in the system currently works—especially the time, costs, and number of steps, all of which should be quantified. This may be presented as detailed flow charts, with descriptions of the steps involved. The flow charts should then be analyzed through a gender lens by exploring the different experiences of men and women using the system. This may be done as part of the data collection process under step 1.1.

A Tracer Study/Secret Shopper approach may also be used. This involves engaging individuals to navigate the registration, licensing, and permitting process,[7] recording all time, authorized and unauthorized procedures, and costs incurred. Engaging both male and female participants in the exercise allows for comparison of their experiences using the system.

Copies of all forms and documents involved in the formalization process should be obtained and analyzed for differences between requirements for women and men applicants. A key issue is whether a woman is required to obtain the signature or consent of her husband or a male relative on application forms.

Where standard methodologies, such as the Compliance Cost Tool and Standard Cost Model, are used to assess the regulatory burden of compliance with licensing and permitting requirements, gender perspectives should be incorporated (see annex B for checklist).

Figure 2.2 gives examples of some of the issues that a gender analysis of a hypothetical business registration process may reveal. Some of the issues revealed may be legal or procedural. Others may be logistical, for example, a recent World Bank Survey of eight Middle East and North African countries revealed that restrictions on women's ability to travel and stay in hotels are major constraints on their ability to formalize their businesses.[8]

As part of the analysis, consideration should be given to whether the services of an intermediary are required formally or as a matter of practice in order to undertake the process. In some countries (for example, Kenya and Uganda) lawyers have a monopoly on company formation—adding to the expense of the process. Ideally, company formation should be so straightforward that it requires no professional assistance (as in New Zealand, where company formation is effected by completion of a simple form requiring basic information). The requirement to retain an intermediary may present a particular barrier for women because they may be less likely than their male counterparts to have access to business networks; they may be less likely to have the time or financial resources to retain a lawyer; or they may face cultural barriers if they seek to consult a male lawyer.

Even where there is no explicit legal or regulatory restriction, cultural or economic norms may force women to depend on men to act as intermediaries with state officials. As a result, women's interactions with officials are less efficient and women's choices are restricted.[9]

2

Figure 2.2	Issues Revealed by a Gender Analysis

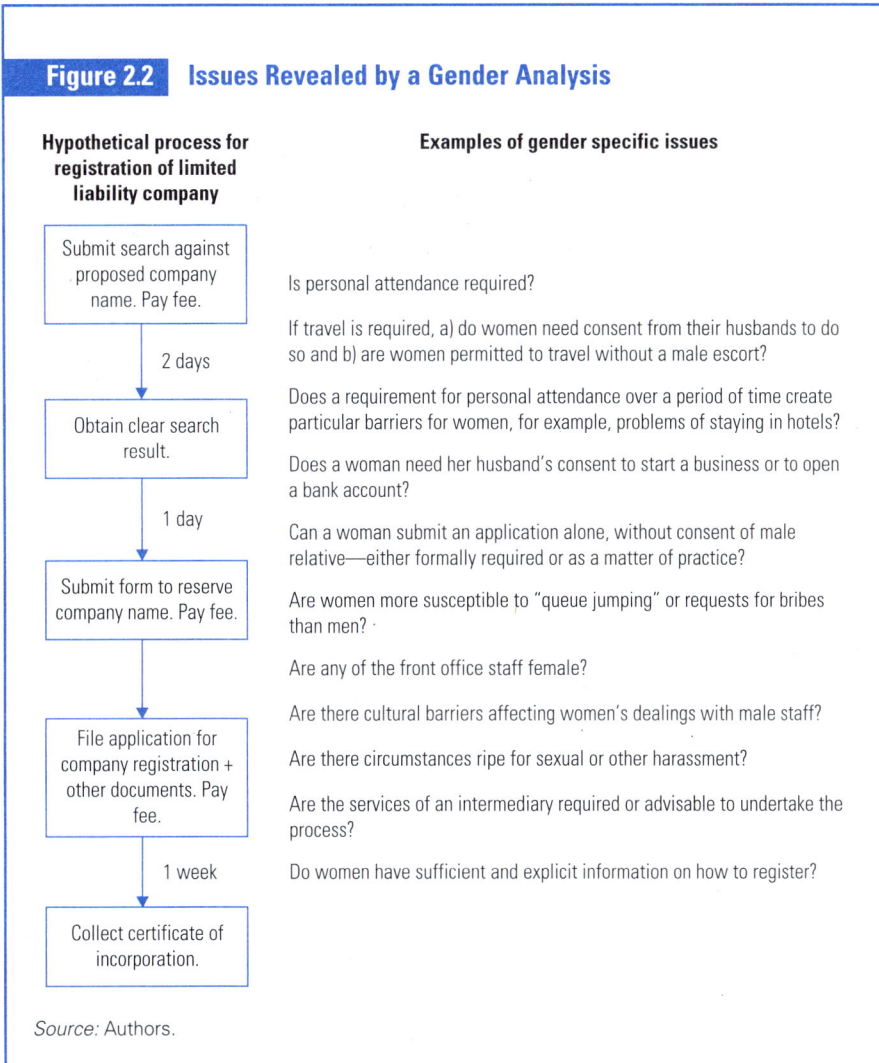

Hypothetical process for registration of limited liability company

Examples of gender specific issues

```
┌─────────────────────┐
│ Submit search against│
│ proposed company    │
│ name. Pay fee.      │
└─────────────────────┘
         │
      2 days
         ▼
┌─────────────────────┐
│ Obtain clear search │
│ result.             │
└─────────────────────┘
         │
      1 day
         ▼
┌─────────────────────┐
│ Submit form to reserve│
│ company name. Pay fee.│
└─────────────────────┘
         │
         ▼
┌─────────────────────┐
│ File application for │
│ company registration +│
│ other documents. Pay │
│ fee.                 │
└─────────────────────┘
         │
      1 week
         ▼
┌─────────────────────┐
│ Collect certificate of│
│ incorporation.       │
└─────────────────────┘
```

Is personal attendance required?

If travel is required, a) do women need consent from their husbands to do so and b) are women permitted to travel without a male escort?

Does a requirement for personal attendance over a period of time create particular barriers for women, for example, problems of staying in hotels?

Does a woman need her husband's consent to start a business or to open a bank account?

Can a woman submit an application alone, without consent of male relative—either formally required or as a matter of practice?

Are women more susceptible to "queue jumping" or requests for bribes than men?

Are any of the front office staff female?

Are there cultural barriers affecting women's dealings with male staff?

Are there circumstances ripe for sexual or other harassment?

Are the services of an intermediary required or advisable to undertake the process?

Do women have sufficient and explicit information on how to register?

Source: Authors.

As well as using such detailed mapping to analyze experiences of men and women when using the system, focusing explicitly on sectors in which women predominate will provide a sound analytical basis for simplifying the processes in these sectors.

1.5   Undertake a Legal Review

The legislation governing formalization procedures should be analyzed for any specific barriers affecting women, such as the requirement for male consent for business registration. In addition, consideration should be given to the wider legal framework, which may affect the ability of women to formalize their businesses. For example, in Lesotho, until recently, women were considered to be legal minors. In Cameroon, under the marriage ordinance, a woman's ability to exercise a trade can be prevented by her husband's objection that it is not in the interests of the marriage or their children. Requirements also may depend on the status of the woman (single, married, divorced, or widowed).

These issues should be considered with respect to the country's international treaty obligations—for example, under the UN Convention on the Elimination of All Forms of Discrimination Against Women (CEDAW)[10]—and with respect to any guarantees of equality contained in the constitution. If legal restrictions on women's ability to formalize their businesses conflict with these overarching obligations, the case for reform may be stronger.

Annex C contains a checklist of legal issues to consider. Local lawyers with appropriate experience, women lawyers' organizations, or NGOs promoting women's rights should be well placed to provide assistance in addressing them.[11]

1.6   Undertake Institutional Assessments through a Gender Lens

When assessing the institutions administering the registration, licensing, and permit regime, the extent to which they have incorporated gender within their operations should be determined. Issues to consider include

- whether the institution has gender-disaggregated data on applications, for example, number of male-owned and female-owned companies registered (if this information is not available, proxy data should be sought, for example, gender-disaggregated samples of applications over the previous period);
- views of key staff in the institution on problems women might face when making an application;
- gender balance of the staff in the organization, particularly those who deal with the public;
- culture of the organization, for example, the extent to which operational manuals, customer charters, and so forth address gender issues (box 2.4); and
- the physical environment of the organization—is it one in which women would feel comfortable?

BOX 2.4   **Assessing the Culture of an Organization**

As well as considering formal or documentary evidence of whether an organization has embraced gender equality in its operations, onsite observations and interviews should be conducted to ascertain the prevailing culture and attitudes. For example, in **Honduras**, despite law reform giving women the same access to land as men, in practice Municipal Land Registers would insist on issuing land titles only to men.

Source: World Bank Legal Department Report 2007.

Step 2   Solution Design

The diagnostic undertaken in step 1 should provide a clear picture of the particular barriers that women face in relation to business entry and operations. Step 2 involves designing solutions to address them.

As has been suggested, the diagnostic may reveal barriers related to the wider social and cultural context that cannot be addressed within the scope of a regulatory reform program.[12] For example, intrahousehold allocation of resources may give women little incentive to formalize: if the husband controls household funds, a woman may prefer to keep her business small and informal, as she would be unlikely to benefit from the increased income that formalization may bring. Regulatory reform programs cannot address this or other underlying social issues,[13] but they can mitigate these forces by developing solutions designed to produce the most enabling environment possible for women and proactively encouraging them to formalize their businesses.

Step 2.1 is the starting point for solution design: a clear determination and agreement of the impact the reforms are seeking to achieve in relation to gender.

The activities to achieve the agreed-on impacts will depend on the barriers to formalization faced by women entrepreneurs identified in the diagnostic phase. Steps 2.2–2.5 provide possible solutions to commonly identified barriers. These are not "one-size-fits-all" solutions, but rather examples of approaches that will need to be adapted for particular contexts.

2.1   Agree on Gender-Related Program Results

The starting point for designing solutions to the barriers identified in the diagnostic is to be clear about what the program is trying to achieve. Clear results relating to women's participation in the formal economy need to be agreed upon by key stakeholders (including women entrepreneurs). Some results (particularly in relation to licensing) may be relevant at the subnational level. Program results may be

- an increase in the number of registered female-owned businesses;
- an increase in the number of first-time female applicants for specified business licenses;[14] or
- an increase in the number of women expressing satisfaction with the registration, licensing, or permit process.

2.2   Undertake Legal and Regulatory Reform to Abolish Discriminatory Provisions

If the diagnostic reveals specific laws or other legal requirements that discriminate against women's business entry and formalization, agreement should be sought to reform or repeal them. It may well be that such laws contravene gender equality provisions in the country's constitution.

2.3 Simplify Processes and Develop Outreach Activities and Communications Strategies to Encourage Women Entrepreneurs to Formalize

Process and regulatory regime simplification are likely to be core program activities (for example, using the "regulatory guillotine"[15] approach). These reforms could include a focus on sectors in which women predominate or may be entirely gender neutral. However, such simplification is likely to give a positively disproportionate benefit to women business owners (box 2.5).

"Women entrepreneurs think they do not need to register their businesses because they have too little income."

— Woman entrepreneur, Kenya

Simplified regimes are more likely to have a positive impact on women if proactive steps are taken to promote them. Strategies could include

- engaging with women's business organizations, NGOs supporting women entrepreneurs, and microfinance institutions lending to women to promote the new procedures and the benefits of formalization in general;

BOX 2.5   Registration and Licensing in Uganda

In **Uganda** a study identified trade licenses as the single most burdensome regulation that small and medium-size firms had to comply with, with 40 percent of women as compared with 30 percent of men citing trade license procedures as an obstacle to business growth.

But just as women reported being more likely to be hindered by cumbersome registration and licensing procedures, they proved more likely to comply with regulations once requirements were simplified. An impact assessment of a successful pilot project to streamline registration procedures in Entebbe Municipality showed that reforms encouraged women to formalize: the increase in first-time business owners registering was 33 percent higher for women than for men.

Source: Uganda Ministry of Finance 2004.

- developing an advertising campaign on formalization aimed specifically at women entrepreneurs (radio may be a particularly effective medium as women may have lower literacy rates than men);
- developing user guides to the registration, licensing, and permit systems aimed specifically at women entrepreneurs (bearing in mind that women may have lower literacy rates than men); and
- providing information kiosks or help desks in key institutions aimed specifically at women's business formalization.

2.4 Address the Licensing Regimes Most Likely to Affect Women Entrepreneurs

The mapping process undertaken under step 1.3 may reveal significantly different licensing regimes for business activities undertaken by women compared with men. If this is the case, when prioritizing areas to be addressed in regulatory reform processes (for example, through better regulation programs where licenses are eliminated or simplified), it will be important that regimes most likely to affect women entrepreneurs be included in the reform process.

2.5 Undertake Institutional Reforms to Provide Improved Service to Women Entrepreneurs

The diagnostic in step 1 includes an interrogation of women's experiences when they interact with the public institutions responsible for registration, licensing, and permits. The diagnostic may reveal specific discrimination faced by women when dealing with these institutions (see box).

Research into public administration in **India** found that women had to wait on average 37 percent longer than men to see the same local government official. Women of roughly the same income as men were three times more likely to be queue-jumped, and 16 percent of women reported sexual harassment from local government officials.[16]

A survey in **Bangladesh** found that government officials are more likely to target female applicants for informal "speed payments" as they are assumed to have a male provider.[17]

Institutional reform of the bodies responsible for registration, licensing, and permits—for example, by the creation of a one-stop shop or a business registration executive agency—is an opportunity to address discriminatory issues. Even in the absence of far-reaching institutional reforms, the following measures can be taken to address gender discrimination:

- Reduce or abolish the need for personal attendance. But careful research will be needed into what form of application would be most accessible for women as well as men. For example, would a Web-based system be more or less accessible to women entrepreneurs?
- Ensure that staff training and operational manuals include gender issues—particularly in relation to customer care.
- Promote a gender balance in the organization, particularly in relation to front office staff.
- Provide dedicated desks or service areas for male and female clients. Consider also whether opening hours are convenient for women.
- Ensure that women customers are aware of service standards applicable to them, including through customer charters, user guides setting out customers' expectations, and clear codes of conduct.

2.6 Ensure That Ongoing Reform Tools Incorporate a Gender Dimension

If such tools as regulatory impact assessments are to be adopted to assess the impact of proposed new licensing or permitting requirements, gender considerations should be included within the methodology (box 2.6).

BOX 2.6 **Regulatory Impact Assessment**

Gender Checklist

- On what data is the proposed measure based? Are the data disaggregated by gender?
- Will men and women each be directly or indirectly affected by the proposed measure?

Sample questions to determine impacts on gender equality:

- Does the measure take into account differences between men and women in access to and use of infrastructure?
- Does the measure take into account the freedom of men and women to dispose of their time?
- Does the measure influence the choice and exercise of an occupation by women and men?
- Does the measure take into account the differences in access to information and education for women and men?
- Does the measure take into account the differences in the daily lives of women and men?

Source: Adapted from *Working Aid: Gender Impact Assessment: Gender Mainstreaming in the Preparation of Legislation* 2007.

Step 3 Implementation and M&E

The general points on implementation and monitoring and evaluation in the core module should be applied to business entry and operation programs. In addition, the following issues should be considered in relation to M&E.

3.1 Ensure Key Information Can Be Gender Disaggregated

Gender-related program impacts should be agreed upon at the start of the solution design process (see step 2.1). For example, gender-disaggregated data on numbers of applications for company registration may be required. But baseline data on key indicators may not be readily susceptible to gender disaggregation (see box). A flexible approach to identifying which businesses are male-headed and which are female-headed will need to be adopted in light of the local business environment and legal structures.

2

> IFC's experience[18] suggests that determining male or female ownership of a business is not straightforward because of the following:
>
> - Data from state registers do not always include the gender of owner.
> - Official statistics can be misleading in terms of real ownership and control. For example, in some jurisdictions companies are required to have a minimum of two shareholders (owners) and directors. This means that even if the business is run by a woman, her husband may also appear on the incorporation application form as coshareholder and/or codirector. Conversely, a woman may be registered as coshareholder or codirector of a family company that is in practice controlled and managed by her husband.
> - The official registers may be out of date.

There could be difficulties even where an application (for a license, for example) may be made by a single person. It will be necessary to ascertain whether this person is necessarily the business owner (as opposed to, say, the manager) and whether data on the gender of the business owners are routinely gathered.

The gathering of gender-disaggregated data on key indicators needs to be undertaken without imposing unrealistic costs and burdens on the project and business entry system:

- Undertake a detailed analysis of current application forms and registers for the information on gender that they yield.
- If new forms or registers are being designed, consider whether it would be appropriate for them to capture data on the gender of the business owner.

2

> **BOX 2.7** **Assessing the Number of Female-Headed Businesses: Experience from the United States and the United Kingdom**
>
> Both the United States and United Kingdom rely on survey evidence to assess the number of female-headed businesses that are operating. In the **United States,** the prime source of information about businesses (including whether they are male- or female-headed) comes from the U.S. Census Bureau's Survey of Business Owners and the Self-Employed.
>
> In the **United Kingdom,** estimates are obtained from three principal sources of data: the Labour Force Survey (which focuses on self-employment); the Global Entrepreneurship Monitor (which focuses on founder-owned businesses); and the Annual Small Business Survey.
>
> *Source:* U.S. Census Bureau 2007.

- If it is not possible or appropriate to incorporate gender disaggregation within the normal registration or application process, consider using sampling techniques—for example, analyzing applications made over a specified time period through interviews and questionnaires (See box 2.7).

3.2 Incorporate Output and Outcome Indicators That Highlight Gender Aspects of the Program

Gender issues should be incorporated within the program's M&E framework at the output and outcome levels. Table 2.1 provides a template for incorporating gender in indicators typically used in business entry and licensing reform programs.

Table 2.1: M&E Indicators

Indicator/Data required	Gender focus (Gender-disaggregation)	Source of data
Output indicators		
• Number of operational manuals produced for training and outreach	• Qualitative indicator: gender-inclusive focus (customer service); gender issues articulated and addressed • Core indicator: Number and/or percentage of men and women participating or benefiting	• Manuals produced • Agency management • Focus group discussions (FGDs) • Interviews with businesswomen
• Workshops and outreach events to disseminate registration, licensing, and permitting requirements and procedures	• Gender disaggregate the participants	• FGDs • Event evaluation forms
Outcome indicators		
• Changes in laws, regulations, and procedures that discriminate against women	• Do women have to obtain husband or other male permission to register, operate, or license a business?	• Legal review • Relevant ministries • Women's business associations
• Average number of days to comply with registration, licensing, and permitting requirements and procedures	• Number of days disaggregated by gender of business owner	• Tracking survey • Agency management • Regulatory impact assessment survey • FGDs • Women's businesses and associations
• Average official cost to comply with registration, licensing, and permitting requirements and procedures • Reduced incidence of corruption	• Cost disaggregated by gender of business owner (to capture corruption or other differences) • Corruption incidence disaggregated by gender of business owner	• Tracking survey • Agency management • Regulatory impact assessment survey • FGDs • Women's businesses and associations
• Number of new enterprises registered in a given period (week, month, year) • Change compared with baseline	• Number and percentage of new enterprises registered over the given period, by gender of business head, manager, or owner[19] • Change compared with baseline disaggregated by gender of business head, manager, or owner	• Registry office • Sample survey

(Continued)

Table 2.1: M&E Indicators (*Continued*)

Indicator/Data required	Gender focus (Gender-disaggregation)	Source of data
Outcome indicators		
• Number of new licenses issued (in priority sectors) in a given period (week, month, year) • Change compared with baseline	• Number and percent of new licenses issued (in priority sectors) over the given period, by gender of business head, manager, or owner • Change compared with baseline disaggregated by gender of business head, manager, or owner	• Licensing office • Sample survey • FGDs • Business associations • Women-in-business forums
• Agency operation and accessibility, ease of mobility, and other restrictions	• Opening hours of registration and licensing agency • Accessible and safe location • Welcoming of women • Percentage of men and women managers or other staff in the agency	• FGDs • Agency management

2

Annex A   Sample Questionnaire for Business Owners

Introduction

1. Type of business: legal form (incorporated, partnership, sole trader, other)
2. Sector or main products
3. Size (number of employees/turnover)
4. Gender of owner(s)
5. Gender of manager(s)

2

> *Note:* The questions below will need to be used flexibly, taking into account the context and level of knowledge and experience of interviewees. Approaches should vary depending on whether the questions are being used in the context of a survey, focus group discussion, or one-on-one interview. Concepts, for example the difference between registration and licensing, may need explanation.
>
> The questions are designed for both informal and formal businesses—but will need to be used flexibly. For example, informal businesses may well have a trading license, even if they are not formally registered, and the questions should be used to probe the procedures and barriers associated with this.

Business Start-Up

1. Is your business registered? [*Note:* Registration requirements vary. Registration is generally with a business registry and/or tax authority.]
2. Does your business have any licenses or permits? [*Note:* Include licenses and permits issued by nation and subnational authorities.]

IF THE ANSWER TO QUESTION 1 OR 2 IS YES, PLEASE ANSWER QUESTIONS 3 THROUGH 19.

3. What licenses or permits is your business required to have? [*Note:* Include licenses and permits issued by national and subnational authorities.]
4. Where did you get the information on how and where to register or obtain necessary licenses or permits?
5. If your business is registered, with whom is it registered?
6. If it is registered, is it registered in your own name? If not, why not?
7. If your business is registered or licensed, did you undertake the registration or licensing process yourself? If someone else undertook the process for you, who was this? Please explain why you used their services.
8. Which license or permit is the most burdensome to obtain?
9. What problems do you encounter when you undertake registration/obtain a [ ] license/obtain a [ ] permit. Please rank in order of severity of the problem.

[*Note:* Specify precisely what process is being referred to. Data are required for each process undertaken.]

- Time consuming
- Expensive
- Demands for bribes
- Harassment by public officials
- Need to travel or stay overnight
- Problems with child care
- Inconvenient opening hours
- Other (please specify)

10. How many days did each process take?

11. How much did each process cost?

12. What were the steps involved in each process?

13. Have you ever been subject to sexual harassment when you have registered or licensed your business?

14. Did you need to seek the permission of a family member (for example, your spouse) before you could register your business or obtain a license for it?

15. When undertaking any of the processes we have been talking about, have you ever been asked for a bribe?[20] Did you give a bribe, and if so, what did you receive in return for it?

16. When you deal with officials in connection with business registration or licensing, with whom do you find it easier to communicate?
    - Women
    - Men
    - No difference

17. Do you consider that you were disadvantaged in any way during the registration or licensing process because of your gender? Do you think the process would have been easier if you had been the opposite gender? If so, how?

18. If your business is registered as a company, are you the sole shareholder or director? If not, who are your coshareholders or directors? Why did you choose not to own the company alone?

19. What improvements in the registration and licensing processes would be of greatest assistance to you and make it easier for you to comply?

IF THE ANSWER TO QUESTION 1 OR 2 IS NO, PLEASE ANSWER QUESTIONS 20 THROUGH 22.

20. Do you know how to register your business or obtain the licenses it needs?

21. Why have you chosen not to register or license your business?

22. What improvements in the registration or licensing process would be of greatest assistance to you and make it easier for you to comply?

QUESTIONS FOR FORMAL AND INFORMAL BUSINESSES

23. What is your perception of the regulatory burden for your business (rank, for example, from light to severe)?
24. What are or would be the benefits (if any) to you of formalizing or registering your business?
25. What are or would be the disadvantages to you of formalizing or registering your business?

2

Annex B Business Licensing Reform: Application of Standard Cost Model and Compliance Cost Tool

Gender Checklist

The Standard Cost Model and the Compliance Cost Tool both provide a quantitative assessment of the costs imposed on businesses by regulation (in this case, by business licenses). Both methods can capture (i) the differential costs on female-headed businesses and male-headed businesses of obtaining a license and (ii) the different experiences of male and female license applicants. This gender-disaggregated information should inform the business licensing reform process.

However, neither method captures two important pieces of information that should inform business licensing reform and policy development:

a) The gender-disaggregated extent of **noncompliance**. International evidence suggests that women may be more likely than their male counterparts to choose not to license their businesses because, for example, of their double time burden, limited knowledge about licensing requirements, or limited business networks. If it is found that women are much less likely than men to license their businesses, the reasons for this need to be investigated (for example, through interviews, focus group discussions, or surveys) and appropriate policy responses developed, for example, targeted information for female-headed businesses.

b) Gender-disaggregated **qualitative costs**. There is international evidence that women are liable to be subjected to sexual harassment when they deal with public officials. This type of experience is not quantifiable, but clearly imposes a significant personal cost on women and is a clear disincentive to comply with licensing requirements. If these qualitative issues are revealed, appropriate policy responses can be developed; for example, if sexual harassment is an issue, assigning female licensing staff to deal with female license applicants.

Noncompliance may be assessed by comparing (i) the total number of license holders with (ii) the total number of businesses. An attempt should be made to find gender-disaggregated data on both (i) and (ii). The licensing authority may have gender-disaggregated information on the proportion of licenses held by male-headed firms and female-headed firms.[21] However, if licenses are in the names of businesses, rather than business owners, this may be problematic. Instead, reliance could be placed on anecdotal evidence from the licensing authority or private sector survey evidence, if available.

Information on **qualitative costs** may be obtained from one-on-one interviews, focus group discussions, or private sector surveys that explore the experience of men and women when they apply for licenses.

Key Aspects Standard Cost Model (SCM)	Key Aspects Compliance Cost Tool (CCT)	Gender perspective	Gender checklist
Provides a framework methodology for measuring *administrative* costs imposed on businesses by government. Aim is to measure the average cost to a business of complying with the regulation.	Provides a framework methodology for measuring *policy* as well as *administrative* costs imposed on businesses by government. Aim is to measure the average cost to a business of complying with the regulation.	If impacts on female-headed and male-headed businesses are assessed separately, both tools will enable differentiated impacts to be revealed and then explored.	• Ascertain proportion of licenses held by female-headed businesses and male-headed businesses (see introduction above for suggestions about how to obtain this information). • Based on the proportions above, use a statistically appropriate number of female-headed firms in the sample frame. For example, if 50% of license holders are female-headed firms, 50% of sample should be female-headed firms. If noncompliance is gender-skewed (for example, women hold far fewer licenses than men): ➢ further analysis should be undertaken to ascertain why this is (see introduction above) and ➢ the gender-disaggregated data should be treated with caution. If few women have obtained licenses, those who have are likely to be untypical (for example, they may be well educated or run large businesses).

(Continued)

Key Aspects Standard Cost Model (SCM)	Key Aspects Compliance Cost Tool (CCT)	Gender perspective	Gender checklist
The administrative burden is measured through in-depth interviews with a small number of firms within the target group of the law. They are asked to specify how much time and money they spend performing each administrative activity that is required when fulfilling a given information obligation. The different effects that a law may have on various types of businesses (or a relevant segment of businesses) is carried out. For example, often it will be necessary to distinguish between smaller and larger firms.	The methodology for measuring both the administrative and policy burdens is as per the SCM, but questions on each type of cost burden are separated so that separate information can be collected on each, and each can be measured separately.	Male and female-headed firms tend to be different—in terms of size and sectors in which they operate.	• The sample should reflect the proportions of male- and female-headed firms of different sizes and in different sectors.
Each administrative activity is a function of the internal and external costs to business, multiplied by the number of times each business has to perform the activity. "Time spent" on fulfilling a requirement is translated into a cost using the wage of the person who is normally assigned to carry out the task, multiplied by the frequency with which that task is carried out.	As per SCM	Even where there is no explicit legal or regulatory restriction, cultural or economic reasons may force women to depend on men to act as intermediaries between themselves and state officials. As a result, women's interactions with officials are less efficient and women's choices are restricted.	• The data should capture the gender of the person assigned to the task of license application and interaction with the public authority concerned. • If the person who obtains the license is not the business owner, the reason(s) for this should be explored, if possible.

Administrative costs are defined as "the costs imposed on enterprises when complying with information obligations stemming from government legislation." Examples include keeping records; carrying out inspections; completing returns and reports; standing in queues to obtain approvals or file documents; entering information in a register; getting hold of a copy of the law to review, reading a brochure about it, or paying a solicitor to explain what one's compliance obligations are; and cooperating with audits or inspections.

Administrative costs are defined as per Standard Cost Model. But it is important to note that they can include costs of *avoiding compliance* with these requirements, including paying bribes to avoid queuing up or to avoid being caught.

The making of unauthorized payments is fertile ground for consideration of gender issues. There is international evidence that firms paying small bribes are likely to spend more management time dealing with officialdom, not less.[22] This imposes a double burden—both the cost of the bribe and the additional management time. But it is unclear whether male- or female-headed firms are more likely to pay bribes:

- Men may be more likely to try to avoid compliance with regulatory requirements than women (for example, by paying bribes). This may be due to their greater exposure to bureaucracy and experience and confidence in dealing with officialdom and that their networks of influence tend to be wider and deeper than those of women entrepreneurs.
- On the other hand, there is international evidence that women are more susceptible than men to queue barging, harassment, and requests for "speed payments," being seen as soft targets.[23]

- Ensure gender-disaggregated data are gathered on unauthorized payments when obtaining a license.
- If possible, gather gender-disaggregated data on costs of avoiding compliance.

2

(Continued)

Key Aspects Standard Cost Model (SCM)	Key Aspects Compliance Cost Tool (CCT)	Gender perspective	Gender checklist
An information obligation is defined as "a compulsory duty to procure or prepare information and subsequently make it available to a public authority or third party."	An information obligation is defined as per SCM. But compliance costs can also include *policy costs*—that is, the cost inherent in meeting the aims of a regulation, for example, a direct cash cost, such as changing stationery to include a tax number; training staff on health and safety compliance and so forth; and paying direct fees, levies, or taxes. Compliance costs can also include the *opportunity cost* (what else could one have been doing or spending one's money on, if the regulation were not there) of complying or not complying with a regulation, although this is notoriously difficult to measure.	Opportunity costs for men and women may be different, as women are more likely to juggle their businesses with family and domestic duties. For a woman, spending less time on a licensing requirement may not necessarily translate into additional time spent attending to her business.	• Gender disaggregate information on opportunity cost (if obtained). Undertake careful analysis in the light of different gender roles.
Enables reduction targets to be set and key areas for reform to be identified.	Enables reduction targets to be set and key areas for reform to be identified.	If gender-disaggregated data are collected, both models will allow a consideration of the different impacts and cost burdens a law may impose on female-headed businesses, as compared with male-headed firms. They will also reveal any differences in the experiences of men and women dealing with public officials in connection with licensing.	• As well as gender disaggregating the data obtained, the reasons behind the differences revealed by the disaggregation should be explored, to enable appropriate policy responses to be developed.

Annex C   Legal Checklist

Note: In each case, identify legal basis (name and date of law or regulation) for answer.

General

1. Are there formal restrictions on the ability of women to run a business that are related to gender? (Consider status of woman—married, single, divorced, widowed)
2. Are women regarded as legal minors?
3. Is the age of majority the same for a woman as for a man?
4. Is polygamy culturally or legally recognized? If so, do second and subsequent wives have lesser rights in relation to running businesses?

2

Incorporated Businesses (registered under Companies legislation)

1. Can women be directors and shareholders of companies in the same way as men?
2. Is the age at which women and men can be directors or shareholders the same?
3. Do women need permission from a male relative or husband in order to be a company director or shareholder?
4. If yes, do men require reciprocal permission?
5. Is there provision in the company law for registration of sole directors and shareholders?
6. Are women permitted to undertake the registration process without involving a man (for example, to accompany then to the registration office)?
7. Is the company registration process the same for women (including married women) as for men? For example, do women have to file additional documents, answer additional questions, go to a different place, or go through additional procedures? Is it different in any way for widowed, divorced, or separated women?
8. Is it necessary or usual to travel (for example, to a town) in order to register a company? If yes, are there any travel restrictions on women?

Unincorporated Businesses (that is, not registered as companies)

1. Is there a registration process for unincorporated businesses (for example, business name registration, registration with tax authorities)?
2. If yes, is such registration compulsory? What is the penalty for noncompliance?
3. Is the age at which women and men can register a business the same?

4. Do women need permission from a male relative or husband to register a business?

5. If yes, do men require reciprocal permission?

6. Are women permitted to undertake the registration process without involving a man (for example, to accompany them to the registration office)?

7. Is the business registration process the same for women (including married women) as for men? For example, do women have to file additional documents, answer additional questions, go to a different place, or go through additional procedures? Is it different in any way for widowed, divorced, or separated women?

8. Is it necessary or usual to travel (for example, to a town) in order to register an unincorporated business? If yes, are there any travel restrictions on women?

Licenses and Permits

1. Are women required to produce additional documents, or undertake additional processes when obtaining licenses for their businesses? (Such provisions may be contained in family laws). What about married, divorced, separated, or widowed women?

2

Notes

1. Registration with a public authority can a) give the business a formal legal identity and/or b) ensure the uniqueness of a company name and/or c) inform the authorities, for example, tax authorities, of the existence of the business. Licensing is taken to mean permissions firms must obtain for their core business activities. Permitting (closely linked to licensing) is permissions for noncore business activities. (See "Business Licensing Reform: A Toolkit for Development Practitioners.")

2. World Bank, *How to Reform*, 18.

3. World Bank Enterprise Surveys.

4. Federacion Internacional de Abogadas (International Federation of Women Lawyers).

5. Section 1.4 also discusses Tracer Studies/Secret Shopper approaches.

6. Listing activities subject to licensing/permits and the laws and regulations that relate to them.

7. See "Business Licensing Reform: A Toolkit for Development Practitioners," 16.

8. Chamlou, "The Environment for Women's Entrepreneurship in the Middle East and North Africa Region," 46.

9. The extent of "male intermediation" is illustrated by the fact that more than a quarter of women in developing countries do not have a say in decisions about their own health care (Progress of the World's Women 2008/2009, UNIFEM).

10. See module 1, section 2.4 for discussion of international treaty obligations.

11. For example, in Cameroon, a local NGO, Women in Alternative Action, has produced a pamphlet detailing laws on the Cameroon statute book that continue to discriminate against women.

12. Discussed in core module.

13. For example, women are likely to be less well educated than men and therefore less aware of formalization processes; they are more likely to have the double time burden of combining their businesses with domestic jobs, and therefore have less time to deal with registration processes.

14. Registration tends to be a one-off event, but licenses usually require renewal.

15. The regulatory guillotine is a means of rapidly reviewing a large number of regulations and eliminating those that are no longer needed. It counts the regulations that exist, and then reviews them against clear criteria, using an orderly and transparent process built on extensive stakeholder input.

16. Corbridge, "Gender, Corruption and the State: Tales from Eastern India," quoted in *The Gender Manual: A Practical Guide* (DFID, 2007).

17. Government of Bangladesh, *Governance, Management, and Performance in Health and Education Facilities in Bangladesh: 2007* (Oxford Policy Management, Financial Management Reform Program, Ministry of Finance).

18. Including in Commonwealth of Independent States and the South Pacific.

19. Collection of gender-disaggregated data from the registry is necessary. However, since is it sometimes difficult to distinguish between ownership and management of a business

2

on the basis of the gender of the applicant, such data need to be interpreted with caution. Where registries do not have company data disaggregated by gender, or where multiple names appear on business registrations, sample surveys and pilot tests may be needed.

20. Include any unofficial payments, such as "speed payments," "facilitation fees," and so forth, including those paid through agents or intermediaries.

21. It will be necessary to identify a working definition of "female-headed/male-headed business." The U.S. Survey of Business Owners and the Self-Employed provides a helpful definition. A female-headed business is at least 51 percent owned by a woman or women and "controlled" by a woman or women ("control" in this context means exercising the power to make policy decisions) and "operated" by a woman or women ("operate" in this context means being actively involved in the day-to-day management).

22. Daniel Kaufman and Shang Jin-Wei. "Does Grease Money Speed up the Wheels of Commerce?" (World Bank, 2000).

23. S. Corbridge, "Gender, Corruption, and the State: Tales from Eastern India," quoted in *The Gender Manual: A Practical Guide* (DFID, 2007). Also Government of Bangladesh, *Governance, Management, and Performance in Health and Education Facilities in Bangladesh: 2007*. (Oxford Policy Management, Financial Management Reform Program, Ministry of Finance).

Business Taxation

This Module Should be Used in Conjunction with the Core Module

This module (i) suggests tools to explore the gender aspects of business taxation[1] (step 1 – diagnostics); (ii) provides possible solutions to ensure that gender issues identified are effectively addressed (step 2 – solution design); and (iii) suggests ways to incorporate gender into implementation and monitoring and evaluation of tax policy and administration reform programs (step 3 – implementation and monitoring and evaluation).

Summary

MODULE 3

Why Gender Matters

Taxation policy (as opposed to tax administration, which is discussed below) includes the statutory basis for taxation—what is taxed and at what rates and who is liable to pay taxes and in what circumstances. In general, women's lower relative earnings and their predominance in informal employment mean that they are unlikely to bear a large share of the personal income or direct tax burden. But indirect taxes, which are a heavier burden on the poor, are likely to have a greater impact on women than on men. Taxation policy can have a fundamental effect on the investment climate, influencing the decisions of businesses and individuals in response to changes in income and relative prices. Behavioral response to changes in tax policy will differ between men and women according to both explicit and implicit biases in the taxation system. For example, decisions made by men and women about the time they spend in formal, informal, and unpaid work are influenced by the impact of taxation on wages and disposable income.

Box 3.1 sets out examples of explicit gender biases, all of which result in disincentives for women to start or grow businesses.

An implicit gender bias arises where the burden of tax is borne disproportionately by women, for example, higher rates of consumption taxes on products and services more commonly consumed or produced by women than men.

3

In **Vietnam** in 2003, there was a range of value-added tax (VAT) rates attributable to different business sectors. In the production sector, predominantly controlled by men, the VAT rate was 5 percent; in the trade sector, where proportionately more women operated, the rate was 10 percent; and in the food and beverage sector, where women predominated, the rate was 20 percent.[2]

BOX 3.1 **Gender Bias in Tax Policies**

In **Tanzania,** family business income is attributed to the husband regardless of the spouse's role in the business.

In **South Africa** before 1995 and in several **Middle Eastern** countries today, the rate of tax applied to married women is higher than to married men.[3]

All **Middle Eastern** countries identify the family, rather than the individual, as the central unit of society. This influences the taxation regime. For example, in **Jordan**, if husband and wife file separately, some tax deductions are available only for the man.

Source: Barnett and Grown 2004.

Such findings should be interpreted with care, however. An implicit gender bias may arise incidentally when there is a valid economic or public policy rationale for a particular tax policy, for example, high "sin taxes" on alcohol and tobacco, which, based on consumption patterns, have greater impact on men than women in most societies.

Evidence from developed countries suggests that married women respond more strongly to the increased incentive of lower tax rates than do men—hence, tax biases *against* women can be particularly economically damaging.

Tax administration includes the procedures for assessment and collection of taxation. Weaknesses in tax administration can also have serious implications for the investment climate, as illustrated by the compliance costs and time to file returns measured by the Doing Business indicators, and may affect female and male entrepreneurs differently. There is clear evidence from developing countries that women are frequently at a disadvantage when dealing with public officials (see box in module 2, section 2.5). This may influence their willingness to register with tax authorities in the first place, and their ability to engage effectively with them once they are registered—for example, where discretion is given to tax administration officials, women may be in a weaker negotiating position than men.

In **Vietnam,** small businesses may be exempted from charging VAT, but are still able to recover input VAT if they are below a threshold size. Businesses need to register to benefit from this exemption. But businesses owned by women are less likely to be registered than businesses owned by men.[4]

BOX 3.2   **Impact of U.S. Tax Reform on Women**

An analysis of the 1986 Tax Reform Act in the **United States**, which lowered the top marginal tax rate from 50 percent to 28 percent, found that married women responded more strongly to the increased work incentive than men did.[5]

Source: Nada 1995.

Step 1   Diagnostics

Step 1 provides tools to analyze whether a country's tax policy or administration contains gender distortions.

> The critical steps to be taken during an initial project design phase (in the absence of a full diagnostic at that point) are identified by a magnifying glass icon. 🔍

1.1   Analyze Tax Policy and Legislation through a Gender Lens

The tax policy framework (generally comprising direct taxes on income and wealth, indirect taxes on consumption, property taxes, and trade taxes) should be reviewed for gender biases, in particular in relation to the tax base. Although the diagnostic focus is on business taxation, this does not mean that only corporate taxes should be considered; in many jurisdictions, unincorporated businesses and sole proprietors are taxed primarily under personal tax regulations, which may include gender biases. For small businesses, it is also important to consider the requirement (if any) for "presumptive taxation" and its impact on cash flow and profitability.

A key gender policy issue is likely to be the tax treatment of married women and the extent to which their income is consolidated with their husband's or family's for tax purposes—the "marriage penalty" (see box 3.3). Any requirement for

3

BOX 3.3   **Marriage Penalty in Tax Codes**

Tax laws in many countries of **Asia** and **Africa** that derive their tax system from English common law are based on the assumption that all the income earned by a married couple is the property of the husband.

The "marriage penalty" occurs when a couple filing joint returns experiences a greater tax liability than would occur if each of the two people were to file as single individuals. Evidence from the **United States**, **Canada,** and **Japan** shows that a system of joint filing results in discouraging secondary workers (usually women) in the household.[6]

The "penalty" may extend beyond wives to other members of the family. In **India** the filing unit for income tax is the Hindu extended family, comprising all male Hindus descended in the male line from a common ancestor and their wives and unmarried daughters.[7]

Source: Esim 2000, Stotsky 2006.

women's taxes to be assessed other than individually increases the relative tax rate on women because when their income is combined, they are effectively taxed at the higher marginal rates.

Annex A contains a checklist of issues to consider.

1.2 Analyze the Tax Burden or Tax Incidence through a Gender Lens

Consideration should be given to whether there is gender bias in the tax burden and tax incidence. Official statistics reflecting gender breakdowns are not readily available, but sample data from tax returns may yield useful information.

> When personal income tax is collected on a joint, as opposed to individual, basis, it can be difficult to obtain gender-disaggregated statistics. If filing is on an individual basis, tax returns may explicitly capture the gender of the filer. Where they do not, gender may be able to be inferred from the name of the filer. Alternatively, a sample of tax returns could be matched to other gender-disaggregated data, for example, social security information.
>
> Gender-disaggregated data are not collected in most countries on indirect taxes.

Questions to consider include the following:

- What proportion of tax is paid by women and what proportion by men?
- What proportion of taxpayers are women and what proportion are men?
- Are sectors in which men and women are engaged subject to different taxation regimes, or different levels of tax take?

In addition, the direct costs of taxes to businesses, *compliance costs* (for example, administrative and logistical expenses and informal payments to officials) should also be considered, especially for smaller businesses, for which these can be a very significant cost. For example, can taxes be paid at a single payment point that is accessible to women? Or does payment of taxes require multiple visits to different offices, where women may experience more difficulties getting served than men? In this regard, the Foreign Investment Advisory Service (FIAS) Tax Compliance and Informality Surveys[8] can provide very helpful context, including experience of corruption in payment of taxes; upcoming surveys should provide gender-disaggregated data.

Consideration should also be given to whether any *tax incentive* regime (that is, special treatment to encourage investment) contains explicit or implicit gender biases. Incentives may be legislated or discretionary to officials or ministers. Discretionary incentives are generally more problematic and may be more prone to implicit gender bias in places where women have less effective access to public officials than men do. Transparency as to what incentives have been provided and on

3

what terms may be poor, although ministries of finance should maintain a register. Although evidence suggests that tax incentives are much less effective than broader socioeconomic and political factors in determining investment rates, there is often strong political pressure for incentives to be given. It may be that beneficiaries tend to be politically well-connected men.

1.3 Review Impact of Local Tax Regime on Women

Many developing countries are implementing decentralization programs, including enhanced revenue-raising powers of local authorities. An understanding of the decentralization process will be required,[9] especially as it relates to local government taxes that may impose a disproportionate burden on businesswomen because

- women are more likely than their male counterparts to operate in the informal or semi-informal sector (see module 2 – Business Entry and Operations);
- women entrepreneurs may be less able to resist the predatory imposition of local taxes (see module 2, section 2.5 with evidence that women tend to be disadvantaged in the dealings with public officials); and
- local government officials may target sectors in which women predominate, such as small-scale market trading, for tax collection.

Consideration should be given to the local tax regime and the extent to which it contains gender biases. For example, the tax structure may be different for sectors in which men predominate versus those in which women do. In addition, local governments should be questioned about the source of their tax take and their collection practices.

Although gender bias in local government taxation may be caused by a deliberate or unintentional policy of the local government itself, it may also arise from the policy framework within which local governments operate, and the limited range of revenue sources that they are permitted to exploit by the central government.

1.4 Obtain Gender-Disaggregated Private Sector Views

Existing private sector surveys (for example, World Bank Enterprise Surveys, Market Surveys, Tax Compliance Surveys) may contain gender-disaggregated data to assist in estimating the relative impact of tax policy and administration on women and men. If published reports do not disaggregate findings on the basis of gender, the raw data may still be available for additional analysis to obtain gender-disaggregated responses.

If a full diagnostic is being undertaken, more in-depth analysis may be required to explore gender differences in tax policy and administration as experienced by the private sector. The pro forma questionnaire for private sector operators in annex B is designed to form the basis for such analysis in the context of (i) one-on-one interviews, (ii) focus group discussions, and (iii) formal surveys. The main focus of the questionnaire is on tax administration, although private sector views are also sought on some tax policy issues.

1.5 Undertake Institutional Assessment through a Gender Lens

Consideration should be given to whether the tax authorities have incorporated gender within their operations. Issues to consider include

- whether the tax authority has gender-disaggregated data on taxpayers;
- the views of the tax authority on problems businesswomen might face when interacting with them;
- the gender balance of the staff in the tax authority, particularly those who deal with the public;
- the culture of the tax authority, for example, the extent to which operational manuals, customer charters, and so forth address gender issues; and
- the physical environment of the tax authority—is it one in which women would feel comfortable?

Step 2 Solution Design

The diagnostic in step 1 may reveal gender distortions in *tax policy* that could discourage women from starting and growing their businesses. For example:

- Sectors in which women are engaged may be more heavily taxed than sectors in which men are engaged.
- Women may be affected by the joint taxation "marriage penalty."
- A highly discretionary tax system (for example, one based on discretionary exemptions) may result in a bias against women.

The key entry point for tax policy reform will be the national budgeting agency—usually the ministry of finance—which will have prime responsibility for ensuring adequate domestic revenue is raised and that the economic incentives are efficient and rational.

The diagnostic may also reveal gender-related inefficiencies in *tax administration* that result in women avoiding engagement with tax authorities or alternatively being subject to discrimination when they do engage.

Step 2 presents solutions to address gender distortions in both tax policy and administration. Step 2.1 provides the rationale for the solutions proposed—a clear agreement as to the intended impact of the reforms. From the perspective of the ministry of finance, revenue impact will be critical here.

2.1 Agree on Gender-Related Program Results

Clear results of proposed reforms to tax policy or administration to remove gender distortions need to be agreed upon by key stakeholders up front. Possible results include

- a taxation regime that is gender and marital status neutral;[10]
- an increase in number of female-owned businesses registered for tax;
- an increase or decrease in amount of tax paid by female-owned businesses; or sectors in which female-owned businesses predominate.

2.2 Undertake Law Reform to Abolish Gender Distortions in Tax Regime

The list that follows contains possible reforms, the appropriateness of which will depend on the specific issues identified in the diagnostic in step 1:

- Repeal laws that prevent married women from separate assessment of their personal income and ensure equal treatments for deductions.

- Consider revision of tax rates to reduce bias against sectors in which women predominate as owners or employees (while taking into account that there may be valid economic or public policy reasons for such tax rates independent of gender considerations).
- Repeal other tax laws that impose a significantly higher tax burden on women or that inhibit women's engagement in economic activities.
- Introduce targeted tax breaks to encourage women's economic participation, such as allowing child care costs as a tax deduction.
- Reduce or eliminate specific tax incentives for investment in favor of broader investment climate reforms, but where incentives remain, ensure they are "gender neutral" both explicitly and in their impact.[11]

2.3   Undertake Capacity Building and Administrative Reform

Increasingly, developing countries are adopting the unified tax authority model, under which one national institution is responsible for all, or most, forms of taxation. This approach can lead to substantial efficiency gains and increases in overall tax collections and provides an entry point for female-oriented service delivery. Measures that could be taken:

- Develop customer charters for tax agencies that are proinvestment and female-friendly.
- Set up taxpayer groups, including women entrepreneurs, to increase cooperation with tax agencies and improve efficiency of collection.
- Train tax agency staff to deal with women taxpayers fairly and efficiently.
- Ensure office locations and opening times are female-friendly.
- Ensure there are sufficient female employees throughout the organization, especially employees who interact with the public.

"Entrepreneurs need to have better access to information. We generally don't have access to information about laws and policies, and the relevant authorities usually aren't forthcoming when enterprises want such information."

— Woman entrepreneur, Vietnam

Step 3 Implementation and M&E

The general points on implementation and monitoring and evaluation in the core module should be applied to tax policy and administration reform programs. In addition the following issues should be considered in relation to M&E.

3.1 Ensure Key Information Can Be Gender Disaggregated

The extensive tools already used for tax policy analysis can be developed to increase their gender focus and obtain gender-disaggregated data. For example, it may be a relatively easy reform to ensure that the gender of tax filers is captured and tax burden analysis includes analysis by gender of the taxpayer.

The **Tanzania** Revenue Authority commissions an Annual Taxpayer Perceptions Survey to identify taxpayer needs. The findings of the survey are not gender-disaggregated.[12]

3.2 Incorporate Output and Outcome Indicators That Highlight Gender Aspects of the Program

Gender issues should be incorporated within the program's M&E framework at the output and outcome levels. Table 3.1 provides a template for incorporating gender in indicators typically used in tax reform programs.

Table 3.1: M&E Indicators

Indicator/ Data required	Gender focus (Gender disaggregation)	Source of data
Output indicators		
• Number of operational manuals produced, • Training and outreach	• Qualitative indicator: gender-inclusive focus (customer service); gender issues articulated and addressed • Core indicator: number and/or percentage of men and women participating or benefiting	• Manuals produced • Agency management • Focus group discussions (FGDs) • Interviews with businesswomen
• Workshops and outreach events to disseminate new tax policy and procedures	• Gender disaggregate the data on participants	• FGDs • Event evaluation forms

(Continued)

Table 3.1: M&E Indicators (*Continued*)

Indicator/ Data required	Gender focus (Gender disaggregation)	Source of data
Outcome indicators		
• Changes in laws, regulations, and procedures that discriminate against women	• Do women have to obtain husband/male permission to engage in business transactions (including paying taxes)?	• Legal review • Relevant ministries • Women's business associations • FGDs
• Change [reduction] in tax rate and widening tax base • Change in number of taxes	• Gender neutrality of tax code • Disaggregate impact of tax reform by gender of business head/ owner/manager • Tax regime "female-friendly?"	• Tax authority • Women's businesses • FGDs • Surveys
• Replacement of tax holidays with investment incentives	• Number and/or percentage of men's and women's businesses benefiting from changes in incentive regime • Extent to which incentive regime is discretionary and whether this has a differential impact on men's and women's businesses.	• Tax authority • Women's businesses • FGDs • Surveys
• Average number of days to comply with tax administration	• Number of days disaggregated by gender of business owner/head/manager	• Tracking survey • Regulatory Impact Assessment Survey • FGD • Women's businesses and associations
• Average official cost to comply with tax administration • Reduced incidence of corruption	• Cost disaggregated by gender of business owner (to capture corruption or other differences) • Corruption incidence disaggregated by gender of business owner/head/manager	• Tracking survey • Regulatory Impact Assessment Survey • FGDs • Women's businesses and associations
• Improvement in tax enforcement and appeal procedures	• Nondiscrimination against women • Extent to which procedures are equally accessible to men and women	

(Continued)

Indicator/ Data required	Gender focus (Gender disaggregation)	Source of data
• User satisfaction with tax policy and administration	• Disaggregate by gender of business owner	• Tracking survey • Regulatory Impact Assessment Survey • Businesses and associations
• Improvements in agency operation and accessibility	• Opening hours of tax administration agency • Accessible and safe location • Welcoming of women • Percentage of male and female managers and staff in the agency	• FGDs • Agency management

3

Annex A   Tax Policy Checklist

Personal Tax

1. What is the tax unit for personal tax purposes (for example, individual, married couple, or extended family)?
2. Does the personal tax code distinguish between men and women in any way (that is, would a woman be taxed differently than a man with the same income)? For example:
   - Are tax deductions equally available to single and to married men and women?
   - Are tax rates the same for single and married men and women?
   - Are there tax credits only available to men or to women, for example, child tax credits?
3. Is there tax provision for multiple wives? If so, is there differential treatment between first and subsequent wives?
4. Are child care costs tax deductible for working women?
5. Are there tax breaks in relation to maternity leave?

Business Tax

1. How is the income of a family business treated for tax purposes? Are microbusinesses owned by women and operating from their homes required to have or eligible for separate tax identification numbers (that is, separate from the household or male income tax identification number)?
2. Does the corporate tax code include tax benefits for female-owned businesses or for businesses employing women?
3. Are there preferential corporate tax rates for industries (such a mining) that employ proportionately more men than women or for industries such as textiles that tend to employ more women?
4. Can female shareholders and directors represent a company for tax purposes in the same way as men?
5. Does the dividend tax code distinguish between men and women?
6. Do labor tax contributions distinguish between men and women?

Property Tax

1. Are different tax rates applied to property depending on the gender of owner?

3

Annex B   Sample Questionnaire for Business Owners

Introduction

1. Type of business: legal form (incorporated, partnership, sole trader, other)
1. Sector/main products
3. Size (number of employees/turnover)
4. Gender of owner(s)
5. Gender of manager(s)

Note: The questions below will need to be used flexibly, taking into account the context and level of knowledge and experience of interviewees. Approaches should vary depending on whether the questions are being used in the context of a survey, focus group discussion, or one-on-one interview.

General

1. To what taxes is your business subject? (Analyze according to level of government that is levying tax, that is, central government or local government.)
   - Tax on business profits
   - Property tax
   - VAT or sales tax
   - Other (Specify which include significant local fees and service charges levied by local governments, municipal, and similar authorities.)
2. On average, how much tax have you paid over the past three years to (i) central government and (ii) local government?
3. What is your perception of the tax burden for your business (rank, for example, from light to severe)?
4. Which tax is the biggest burden for your business and why? (Analyze according to level of government that is levying tax, that is, central government or local government.)
   - Tax on business profits
   - Property tax
   - VAT/sales tax
   - Other (specify)
5. What improvements in the taxation system or administration would be of greatest assistance to you and make it easier for you to comply?

Central and Local Government Taxation

6. Do you file a tax return on your own account, or is it consolidated with your spouse's or family's?

7. When paying tax do you need to visit an office? If yes—
   - How many visits have you paid in the past three years?
   - What was the purpose of those visits?
   - Describe your experience during the visits.
   - Did you deal with an official of the same gender as you? If not, would you have preferred to?
   - What was the outcome of your visit? Would you describe it as satisfactory?

8. What problems do you encounter when you pay tax? Please rank in order of severity of the problem, and give details of the problem.
   - Lack of transparency about demands for payment
   - Frequency of demands for payments
   - Demands for bribes or other informal payments
   - Harassment by public officials
   - Other (please specify)

9. Have you ever been subject to sexual or other harassment by a tax-collection official? Please give details. Do you think the problem was made worse by the fact of your gender?

10. When paying taxes, have you ever been asked for a bribe[13] (for example, an unofficial payment in return for a reduction in tax)? Did you give a bribe, and if so, what did you receive in return for it? Estimate total amount of bribes and similar informal payments paid annually in relation to tax, analyzed, if possible, between local and central government taxes.

3

Notes

1. Business income is in many circumstances taxed as personal income and to this extent, this module considers also personal tax.

2. Irene Van Staveren and A. Haroon Akram-Lodhi, "*A Gender Analysis of the Impact of Indirect Taxes on Small and Medium Enterprises in Vietnam.*" (The Hague, The Netherlands: Institute of Social Studies, 2003).

3. All examples in box are taken from Barnett and Grown, *Gender Impacts of Government Revenue Collection: The Case of Taxation* (London: Commonwealth Secretariat, 2004).

4. Van Staveren, et al., op. cit.

5. Eissa Nada, "Taxation and Labour Supply of Married Women: The Tax Reform Act of 1986 as a Natural Experiment" (Cambridge, MA: National Bureau for Economic Research, 1995).

6. Simel Esim, "Impact of Government Budgets on Poverty and Gender Equality," 2000.

7. Janet Stotsky, "Gender bias in tax systems," *Tax Notes International,* 1997.

8. To read more about the Foreign Investment Advisory Service (FIAS) Tax Compliance and Informality Surveys, see http://www.fias.net/ifcext/fias.nsf/Content/Pubs_Business Taxation?OpenDocument&StartPagePublicationsbyProductLinesBusinessTaxation=2.

9. Understanding the country's decentralization program is also critical for other *Practitioners' Guide* modules, especially module 2 (Business Entry and Operations).

10. Possibly subject to targeted tax breaks related to child care and maternity leave to encourage women's economic participation. These arguably result in a more equitable sharing of the costs of reproduction between women and men.

11. The tax break proposed in the bullet point is aimed at equalizing the impact of child care across society and redressing an existing imbalance.

12. A. Ellis, M. Blackden, J. Cutura, F. MacCulloch, H. Seebens, 2007. *Gender and Economic Growth in Tanzania: Creating Opportunities for Women*, Directions in Development, World Bank, Washington, D.C.

13. Use term only if culturally appropriate—otherwise "speed payment," "facilitation payment," and so forth, per note in previous module.

3

Trade Logistics

This Module Should be Used in Conjunction with the Core Module

Efficient, easy, and accountable import and export procedures have a significant impact on the business environment. Initiatives to improve trade logistics typically aim to (i) simplify and harmonize procedures and documentation; (ii) implement electronic processing and automation and develop single-window systems; (iii) introduce risk management in border inspections and clearance; and (iv) build capacity to improve efficiency in customs and technical control agencies.

This module (i) provides tools to identify trade logistics constraints that have a disproportionate impact on women (step 1 – diagnostics); (ii) provides possible solutions to ensure that gender issues identified are effectively addressed in initiatives to improve trade logistics (step 2 – solution design); and (iii) suggests ways to incorporate gender into implementation and monitoring and evaluation of trade logistics reform programs (step 3 – implementation and monitoring and evaluation).

Summary

MODULE 4

Why Gender Matters

Efficient trade logistics systems and services have the potential to increase trade—and thus growth, private investment, and jobs. To reap maximum benefits from trade logistics reforms, barriers that affect women, as well as those that affect men, must be addressed.

There is extensive (and conflicting) literature on the impact of trade and globalization on women.[1] What is clear is that women in developing countries are massively involved in export sectors, such as agriculture (where they typically comprise about 50 percent of the workforce) and in labor-intensive manufacturing, including electronics assembly and textiles. In Bangladesh, for example, women comprise 90 percent of the 1.8 million workers in the export-oriented textile sector.[2]

Women not only participate in international markets as workers, they are also importers and exporters in their own right (box 4.1).

But, generally, women's businesses, which tend to be small and concentrated in the informal sector, are not well placed to participate in international trade, because of social and cultural factors, for example, (i) inequalities in access to resources (land, finance[3]) as well as lower levels of education and social restrictions; (ii) domestic work, such as child care and household management; and (iii) inability to own land. Trade logistics programs are not able to address these broader issues relating to women's access to international trade. What they can do, however, is ensure that businesswomen who are involved in importing and exporting reap the

4

BOX 4.1   Women as Importers and Exporters

In **Tunisia,** a World Bank-supported program that provides financial and technical assistance to exporters (FAMEX) partners with the National Businesswomen Association (CNFCE) and ENDA, a microcredit provider for women, on providing export development assistance to women business owners. The partnership is anchored in an agreed work plan and monitorable deliverables between FAMEX and the associations. This assistance includes education, technical support with export development plans and trade fairs, and export finance. This has been viewed as most valuable by businesswomen consulted. CNFCE has recognized the achievements of its members in international markets through the production of a video highlighting success stories.

In the **Windward Islands,** the banana sector has been a traditional export crop, mainly because of preferential European Union treatment. A large majority of the banana producers are women, about 40 percent of whom are single heads of households.[4]

(Continued)

> **BOX 4.1**   **Women as Importers and Exporters (*Continued*)**
>
> In **Kenya,** the Women Entrepreneurs for Industrial Growth Project (supported by the United Nations Industrial Development Organization [UNIDO]) provides technical and managerial training services to women entrepreneurs involved in textiles and related products. Forty percent of the women trained are now exporting to African, European, and U.S. markets.
>
> In **Nicaragua,** UNIDO is working with milk and cheese producers in the neighboring provinces of Boaco and Chontales. As a result of the cluster development, producers are now exporting their cheese to El Salvador and Honduras. About one-third of the exporting enterprises are managed by women.
>
> In a survey of women's businesses in the **Middle East and North Africa,**[5] between one-quarter and one-half of women surveyed were trading internationally.
>
> *Sources:* Robinson 2001; IFC GEM 2007.

4

same benefits from improvements in import and export processes as their male counterparts. If women are able to benefit from trade logistics reform and simplification, they may reap greater benefits from it than their male counterparts (see box).

> Reducing the time goods spend in transit frees up firms' working capital. Female-headed firms tend to have lower working capital than male-headed firms (both because their businesses tend to be smaller and because they may have less access to finance). A reduction in transit time for goods may therefore benefit women's firms more than men's.

Step 1   Diagnostics

Key trade logistics issues commonly constraining trade in developing countries include complex and cumbersome regulatory policies and procedures, uneven application of tariffs and fees, inefficient border control and inspection regimes, and burdensome documentation. Step 1 provides tools to analyze to what extent these types of barriers affect men and women.

The critical steps to be taken during an initial project design phase (in the absence of a full diagnostic at that point) are identified by a magnifying glass icon. 🔍

1.1   Obtain Gender-Disaggregated Private Sector Views

There is emerging evidence that trade logistics barriers are not only different for women entrepreneurs, but also more severe. Research undertaken across Africa[6] shows how lack of physical security at borders differentially affects women, who report a high incidence of physical assaults at border areas. Because women are more likely to operate outside mainstream business circles or have more limited business networks, accurate trade information on regulations, administrative rulings, and general customs requirements does not reach them (see box 4.2). Women are also more likely to face limited access to credit,[7] which hampers their ability to pay customs and related fees. In the case of small-scale cross-border trading, women traders have low levels of literacy. For this reason, as well as for cultural reasons, they tend to depend on brokers or agents to transact business and clear goods. Brokers have been reported to make women pay nonexistent taxes—even on duty-free goods—eroding their profit margin.

Existing private sector surveys (for example, Investor Roadmaps, Investment Climate and Enterprise Surveys, and Compliance Cost Surveys may be a starting point for considering these issues. They may contain gender-disaggregated data on the perceived nature and severity of procedural barriers to import and export. If published reports do not disaggregate findings on the basis of gender, the raw data may still be available for additional analysis.

More in-depth analysis may be required to explore differences in the experience of men and women importers and exporters. The pro forma questionnaire for private sector operators in annex A is designed to reveal differences in trade logistics constraints faced by women and men. The questionnaire can form the basis of (i) one-on-one interviews, (ii) focus group discussions (FGDs), and (iii) formal surveys.

Business associations, particularly those representing importers and exporters, may be male dominated. Trade logistics programs commonly use chambers of commerce to distribute questionnaires about trade logistics constraints among their members. Care should be taken to ensure that women are included in the

4

> ### BOX 4.2   Constraints to Business Growth
>
> A World Bank Urban Informal Sector Investment Climate Analysis in **Kenya** in 2006 surveyed 250 firms in Nairobi and its environs. The survey revealed that, on average, women perceive tax rates, tax administration, and customs to be greater constraints to business growth than do men.
>
> In **Tanzania,** interviews with women entrepreneurs revealed that negative attitudes and intimidation by government officials are a major issue in their interactions with port officials. For women, key concerns are the potential for abuse of wide discretionary powers. Women tend to have less exposure to and experience dealing with officialdom than their male counterparts, as well as fewer networks of influence in government circles. Therefore they are less confident when confronted with corrupt or intimidating behaviour on the part of officials than are their male counterparts. Even with automation, opportunities for manipulation remain, for example, in querying valuations or demanding costly extra physical inspections. Women interviewed also lamented a lack of clear information on rights and obligations, which makes them vulnerable to exploitation, poor enforcement behavior by officials, and poor service attitudes by tax officials.
>
> *Sources:* Ellis et al 2007.

4

questioning, as they may not be members or may not form a significant percentage of the membership.

Efforts should be made to engage with females involved in international trade—for example, through business development projects to open access to markets and through women's business associations. If there is a local chapter of the Organization of Women in International Trade,[8] it may be of assistance. Annexes of the core module and module 1 contain checklists of issues to bear in mind when seeking the views of women entrepreneurs.

It has been observed that women do not take part in stakeholder roundtables. Even if invited, they may come once but not return for future meetings. When they do attend, they are also less likely to raise constraints and problems, and it is therefore difficult to identify their particular constraints.

1.2   Map Existing Processes through a Gender Lens

Obtaining a clear understanding of what the current processes are and how they work is critical before moving on to solution design. Current processes should be mapped, showing the agencies, documents, and fees involved in the process, and the time and cost of import and export procedures quantified—through a gender lens (see table 4.1). This means, at a minimum, ensuring that informants include both male and female users of the system, in discussions with user groups and one-on-one interviews. As suggested in relation to business entry and operations (module 2), a more sophisticated approach would be to conduct a Tracer/Secret Shopper Study (see module 2, section 1.4) comparing the different experiences of men and women. Potential issues that may be revealed include

- the particular difficulties and discrimination that women frequently face when dealing with male public officials—for example, in customs sheds when required to verify the load after a shipment has been screened and a possible misdeclaration found (see box in module 2, section 2.5); and
- problems in obtaining letters of credit, which may be more difficult for women than for men.

1.3 Undertake Institutional Assessment through a Gender Lens

An institutional assessment of the authorities administering the system (which will include port and customs officials) should be undertaken to assess the extent to

4

Table 4.1: Trade Logistics in Rwanda

Example: Rwanda—time to import		Examples of gender specific issues:
SEA		Degree of negotiation required? Are there barriers to women negotiating?
	7 days	
MOMBASSA PORT		Is there gender balance of public officials involved in the process?
	10 days	
MOMBASSA PORT GATE		Are there cultural barriers to women dealing with male staff?
	5 days	
MALABA (KENYAN BORDER)		
	2 days	Are women more susceptible to queue jumping or requests for bribes than men?
MALABA (UGANDAN BORDER)		
	2–3 days	
KATUNA (UGANDAN BORDER)		Are there opportunities for sexual or other harassment?
	1 day	
RWANDAN BORDER		Do women face information disadvantages that increase the costs in time and money of customs processing?
	2–4 hours	
DRY PORT (KIGALI)		
	2–3 days	
DRY PORT GATE		Does the process produce time constraints that differentially have a negative impact on women (for example, transactions that extend into the night or length of transactions that conflict with women's family responsibilities)?

Documentation and prearrival procedures: 25 days. More than 50 percent of time accounted for by regulatory procedures.

Are additional licenses, permits, or fees required for specific sectors in which women's imports or exports tend to dominate?

Source: From IFC's trade logistics process mapping program in Rwanda.

which they have incorporated gender issues within their operations. Issues to consider include

- whether there are gender-disaggregated data on users of the system;
- the views of the institution on problems businesswomen might face when interacting with them;
- the gender balance of the staff in the institution, particularly those who deal with the public;
- the culture of the institution: (i) assess the extent to which operational manuals, customer charters, and so forth, address gender issues and (ii) conduct on-site observations to assess the extent to which the culture is gender neutral; and
- the physical environment of the institution—is it one in which women would feel comfortable?

4

Step 2   Solution Design

Step 2 sets out practical measures for ensuring that gender considerations are fully taken into account when designing solutions to trade logistics constraints to ensure that the needs of women as well as men are addressed. The starting point is for all stakeholders to agree on the gender impact that the reforms are intended to have.

2.1   Agree on Gender-Related Program Results

The key result that trade logistics programs are intended to achieve is, ultimately, increased trade and thus private investment, growth, and jobs. An appropriate indicator, such as that suggested in section 3.2, should be agreed upon not only by the public authorities involved in the reform program but also by women entrepreneurs, particularly with women's business associations or other organizations involved with women importers and exporters.

2.2   Ensure Reforms Are Accompanied by a Communications Strategy Aimed at Women Entrepreneurs

4

A number of factors can prevent women's participation in international trade. If improved procedures are to improve women's ability to access international markets, proactive measures targeted at women will likely be needed to encourage women to consider broadening the scope of their businesses. A communications strategy should be developed in partnership with organizations or initiatives working with female importers and exporters. This could include such things as

- promoting the benefits of the improved procedures and the message that trade is for women as well as men; and
- developing user guides to the new procedures that are specifically targeted at women (for example, any pictures should include women traders as well as men).

2.3   Undertake Institutional Reforms to Provide Improved Service to Women Entrepreneurs

Trade logistics programs usually involve significant institutional reform, process reengineering, and capacity building for the institutions administering the system (customs, port authorities, and technical control agencies). This typically involves reform of procedures and documents, including using automation (using appropriate and accessible technology) and a single window. These types of reforms are an opportunity to address gender discrimination that may be unrecognized and yet systemic in the operations of the organization. Precise interventions should be designed in close consultation with women's business associations. These could include

- developing customer charters for agencies that explicitly address gender issues and problems in service delivery to women;
- ensuring standard training, operational manuals, and codes of conduct include gender issues, particularly in relation to customer care;
- promoting a gender balance in the organization, particularly in relation to front office staff; and
- providing dedicated service points for female clients.

2.4   Design Risk Management Systems to Enable Women to Benefit

Emerging evidence indicates that women tend to be more compliant than men, and therefore female-headed firms stand to gain particular benefit from the installation of a risk-management system for inspections (see box). Female-headed firms may be more likely to be labeled as low risk and so will experience fewer inspections and a faster processing time through customs. The fact that female-headed firms tend to be more compliant could be one parameter that is used to develop and refine the risk management system if gender-disaggregated data are collected from the users on the standard customs forms.

Risk management involves developing and refining, by data feedback, a system whereby both individual users and shipments can be preidentified as low risk (green), medium risk (amber or yellow), and high risk (red). According to international best practice green channel goods are not inspected, yellow channel goods undergo documentary inspection while red channel implies both documentary and physical inspection.

4

Step 3   Implementation and M&E

The general points on implementation and monitoring and evaluation in the core module should be applied to trade logistics reform programs. In addition, the following issues should be considered in relation to M&E.

3.1   Ensure Key Information Can Be Gender Disaggregated

An assessment should be made of the extent to which basic information collected by customs, port authorities, and so forth, is capable of disaggregation on the basis of gender. Key data include customer satisfaction levels and statistics on import and export time and cost. There will be complexities in gender disaggregation—for example, distinctions will need to be drawn between female-owned and female-managed businesses and between women dealing in person with the import and export procedures and those dealing through an employee or representative.

3.2   Incorporate Output and Outcome Indicators That Highlight Gender Aspects of the Program

4

Gender issues should be incorporated within the program's M&E framework. Table 4.2 provides a template for including gender in indicators typically used in trade logistics reform programs.

Table 4.2: M&E Indicators

Indicator/Data required	Gender focus (Gender disaggregation)	Source of data
Output indicators		
• Agency operation and accessibility	• Opening hours of customs, ports, and other trade logistics agencies • Accessible and safe locations • Welcoming of women • Percentage of men and women managers and staff in the agency	• FGDs • Agency management
• Number of operational manuals produced • Training and outreach	• Qualitative indicators: gender-inclusive focus (customer service); gender issues articulated and addressed • Core indicator: number and/or percentage of men and women participating or benefiting	• Manuals produced • Agency management • FGDs • Interviews with businesswomen

(Continued)

Table 4.2: M&E Indicators (*Continued*)

Indicator/Data required	Gender focus (Gender disaggregation)	Source of data
• Knowledge of trade logistics, requirements, and procedures	• Ascertain level of knowledge of both men and women of these requirements and procedures	• FGDs • Agency management, • Women's business associations • Sample surveys
• Mobility and other restrictions	• Do women have to obtain husband or other male permission to engage in business transactions (including trade)? • Is travel involved? If so, are there restrictions on women's travel, such as husband's or other male's permission?	• FGDs • Women's business associations • Women's legal rights • Nongovernmental organizations • Country legal and social analysis
Outcome indicators		
• Average number of days to comply with trade logistics requirements (separate assessment of number of procedures and documents required by customs and technical agencies, for example, port, health, standards bureau)	• Number of days disaggregated by gender of business owner	• Tracking survey • Agency management • Regulatory Impact Assessment Survey • FGDs • Women's businesses and associations
• Average official cost to comply with trade logistics requirements • Reduced incidence of corruption	• Cost disaggregated by gender of business owner (to capture corruption or other differences) • Corruption incidence disaggregated by gender of business owner	• Tracking survey • Agency management • Regulatory Impact Assessment Survey • FGDs • Women's businesses and associations
• Percentage of containers physically inspected	• Number and/or percent of containers disaggregated by gender of business owner	• Agency management • FGDs • Women's businesses and associations

4

Annex A   Sample Questionnaire for Business Owners

Introduction

1. Type of business: legal form (incorporated, partnership, sole trader, or other)
2. Sector or main products
3. Size (number of employees and turnover)
4. Gender of owner(s)
5. Gender of manager(s)

Note: The questions below will need to be used flexibly, taking into account the context and level of knowledge and experience of interviewees. Approaches should vary depending on whether the questions are being used in the context of a survey, focus group discussion, or one-on-one interview.

Trade Logistics

Questions for firms that are involved in importing or exporting:

1. Do you deal with import or export procedures and authorities yourself? If not, who does this on your behalf?
2. If you use an intermediary, please explain why.
3. Are you satisfied with the service the intermediary provides? Please explain why or why not.
4. What is your perception of the service provided by each of the authorities you deal with in connection with importing and exporting? Pick the most appropriate response for each authority:
   - Very helpful and facilitative
   - Quite helpful and facilitative
   - Not at all helpful and facilitative
   - Obstructive
5. What problems do you encounter in relation to import or export procedures? Please rank in order of severity of the problem:
   - Time consuming
   - Expensive
   - Demands for bribes
   - Harassment by public officials
   - Requirement for lengthy periods of attendance
   - Other (please specify)
6. How many days on average does it take to complete import or export formalities?

4

7. How much time on average do you spend on completing import or export formalities?
8. What were the steps involved in each process?
9. Have you ever been subject to sexual harassment when dealing with import or export authorities?
10. When undertaking import or export processes, have you ever been asked for a bribe?[9] Did you give a bribe, and if so, what did you receive in return for it?
11. What is your perception of the availability of information required to efficiently complete the import or export formalities? Pick the most appropriate response for each authority:
    - Extensive and sufficient
    - Adequate
    - Not easily accessed
12. What improvements in the import or export process would be of greatest assistance to your business?

4

Notes

1. For summaries see, for example, Tran-Nguyen and Zampetti (eds.), *Trade and Gender: Opportunities and Challenges for Developing Countries* (UNCTAD, Geneva); ODI, "Untangling the Links Between Trade, Poverty and Gender" (ODI, 2008). Increased trade has the potential to benefit women by (i) increasing female penetration of the formal labor market due to disproportionate growth of female employment in export-oriented, labor-intensive light manufacturing; and (ii) resulting in lower priced goods and services because of increased import-induced competition. On the other hand, it is suggested that women may be more vulnerable than men to negative effects of trade liberalization and less able to benefit from positive impacts.

2. Ibid., 150.

3. Most studies find that women are not more likely than men to be rejected for loans or be subject to higher interest rates (although there is plenty of anecdotal evidence of discriminatory attitudes on the part of financial institutions). But women are less likely to apply for loans than men. (See World Bank, 2007, *Millennium Development Goals Global Monitoring Report,* Washington, DC, 110).

4. N. Robinson, "Small Island States Caught Between Elephants and Hippos" (paper prepared for a Women and Development workshop, 27 October 2001).

5. Surveys conducted by IFC GEM in Bahrain, Jordan, Lebanon, Tunisia, and the United Arab Emirates in 2006. *Women Entrepreneurs in the Middle East and North Africa: Characteristics, Contributions and Challenges.*

6. S. A. Peberdy, "Border Crossings: Small Entrepreneurs and Cross Border Trade Between South Africa and Mozambique," *Journal of Economic and Social Geography* 91(4): 361–378; Y. Dejene, "Women's Cross-Border Trade in West Africa." *WIDTECH Information Bulletin,* 2001; Friedrich Ebert Stiftung and Collaborative Centre for Gender and Development, "Women and Cross Border Trade in East Africa: Opportunities and Challenges for Small Scale Women Traders," 2006.

7. See footnote 3.

8. To read more about the Organization of Women in International Trade (OWIT), see http://www.owit.org/en/Home/Index.aspx.

9. Include any unofficial payments such as "speed payments," "facilitation fees," and so on, including those paid through agents or intermediaries.

4

Secured Lending

This Module Should be Used in Conjunction with the Core Module

This module provides tools to enhance reforms to improve women's ability to use movable assets as collateral for loans.

The module (i) suggests methods to explore differences in women's and men's access to secured lending (step 1 – diagnostics); (ii) provides possible solutions to enable women to benefit from programs of secured lending reform (step 2 – solution design); and (iii) suggests ways to incorporate gender considerations into implementation and monitoring and evaluation of secured lending reform programs (step 3 – implementation and monitoring and evaluation).

Summary

MODULE 5

Why Gender Matters

Lack of access to finance is consistently cited by business owners as one of their most limiting constraints, and it disproportionately affects women (box 5.1). Most studies find that women are not more likely than men to be rejected for loans or be subject to higher interest rates. But women are less likely to apply for loans than men.[1]

> *"Sometimes it's difficult when you're a woman. You don't have property to give as security for financing. I am getting financing from a women's group, not from banks."*
>
> — Woman entrepreneur, Kenya

Microfinance has made a major contribution to enhancing women's access to credit: it is estimated that 8 out of every 10 microfinance clients are women.[2] But the rigidities of microfinance can be limiting for women. By definition, amounts lent are small; interest rates tend to be higher than commercial bank rates; and lending periods are short.

Lack of access to land title can be a major impediment for both men and women seeking finance in formal systems that are frequently highly collateralized. But the problem is likely to be significantly worse for women (see box 5.1).

> *It's almost like they [the banks] are in the property business, not finance.*
>
> — Woman entrepreneur, Kenya

5

Reforms of a country's secured lending system to enhance the use of movable securities can have a significant impact on access to credit across the board (see box 5.3).

BOX 5.1 **Collateral Requirements in Kenya**

More than 85 percent of loans in **Kenya** require collateral. The average value of the collateral taken is nearly twice that of the loan. In the vast majority of cases, the collateral required is land, usually land that has a registered title. Women hold only 1 percent of registered land titles, with about 6 percent of registered titles held in joint names.

Sources: World Bank, Kenya Investment Climate Survey, 2004.

BOX 5.2 Lack of Access to Finance

Although women entrepreneurs run nearly half of **Kenya**'s micro, small, and medium enterprises, they receive less than 10 percent of credit. And they receive only 1 percent of credit directed to agriculture, despite managing 40 percent of smallholder firms.

Women in **Uganda** own about 40 percent of their country's private enterprises, but receive only 9 percent of credit.

In **Tanzania,** nearly 30 percent of male-headed enterprises have received bank finance, whereas only 8 percent of female-headed enterprises have. Only 10 percent of men are currently bank-financed; the proportion of women is half that.

In a survey of women's businesses in the **Middle East and North Africa**, most women owners did not have access to formal credit and were financing their businesses mainly through personal sources, such as savings, family and friends, and by reinvestment of their business earnings.

Sources: Ellis, 2006 and 2007; IFC GEM 2007.

5

BOX 5.3 Impact of Secured Lending Reforms

In 1999 **Romania** undertook a package of measures, including legal reform, to make it easier for a wider range of movable assets to be used as collateral. Since then, more than 200,000 notices of security interests have been registered, the number of borrowers has increased threefold, and the volume of credit by 50 percent.

Following similar reform in the **Slovak Republic** in 2002, more than 70 percent of new loans to businesses are now backed by movable assets and receivables. Credit to the private sector has since increased by 10 percent.

Source: World Bank, Doing Business in 2006.

Enabling movable assets—such as machinery, book debts, jewelry, and other household objects—to be used as collateral can benefit all businesses. But opening up this type of financing has the potential to be of particular benefit to land-poor women, enabling them to circumvent their lack of titled land and use the assets they do have to unlock access to formal credit markets (see box).

> **BOX 5.4** **Use of Movable Assets as Collateral**
>
> In **Sri Lanka,** women commonly hold wealth by way of gold jewelry. This is accepted by formal banks as security for loans.
>
> In **Tanzania,** Sero Lease and Finance, a women's leasing and finance company provides loans to women to purchase equipment for their businesses, using the equipment as security through leasing agreements.[3] Sero has more than 10,000 exclusively female clients.
>
> *Source:* M.S. Pal 1998, Ellis (et al) 2008.

Women's access to credit not only enables them to start or grow their businesses, but the impact on the household is likely to be profound. When poor women (rather than men) are the direct beneficiaries of credit, its impact on the various measures of household welfare (such as school enrollment rates[4]) is greater.

5

Step 1   Diagnostics

Step 1 provides tools to explore (i) the extent to which patterns of secured lending are skewed in favor of men[5] and (ii) legal, regulatory, and administrative reasons for any such unequal distribution.

> The critical steps to be taken during an initial project design phase (in the absence of a full diagnostic at that point) are identified by a magnifying glass icon. 🔍

1.1   Analyze the Lending Market through a Gender Lens

Key issues to assess:

- How important is collateral in the lending system? What percentage of lending requires collateral?
- What percentage of (secured) lending is to women and what percentage to men?
- What percentage of collateral taken is land title and what percentage is movable[6] assets?
- What percentage of registered land title is held by women?

Possible sources for this information may include the central bank, the national statistics office, the ministry of land or land registry (in relation to the question about land), and reports on the financial sector.

If a full diagnostic is being undertaken, overall information on the lending market could be supplemented by more detailed exploration of the issues with officials from commercial banks and other lending institutions. Annex A contains a checklist of key questions to ask.

There may be organizations in the country that provide secured finance primarily or exclusively for women—such as microfinance institutions, savings and loan cooperatives, or banks with credit lines directed at female-owned businesses (for example, Access Bank in Nigeria—see box). These organizations may have interesting perspectives on women's ability to access secured lending generally and on the more specific questions in Annex A.

> Access Bank, one of **Nigeria**'s leading banks, is one of the first banks in Africa to dedicate lines for credit to finance female-owned businesses. IFC provided the bank with a US$15 million loan, specifically to extend lines of credit to women entrepreneurs. In addition, IFC provided comprehensive assistance and training to the bank to enhance its ability to reach out to the women's market.

5

1.2 Obtain Gender-Disaggregated Private Sector Views

a) **Consider existing private sector surveys for gender-disaggregated data.**

Gender disaggregation of existing data may reveal differences in men's and women's abilities to access finance or secured lending and the reasons for any such differences. Good sources of information are likely to include Finscope™ Surveys,[7] investment climate surveys, household surveys, and enterprise surveys. The central bank may also have conducted relevant research and have survey information. If a published report does not contain gender-disaggregated data, it may be possible to access the underlying data (particularly if the research has been conducted recently), which may be susceptible to gender disaggregation.

National and international nongovernmental organizations (NGOs), particularly those with a focus on gender (which may not traditionally be consulted in investment climate work) should also be requested to provide any relevant survey evidence they may have.

b) **Collect new data from the private sector.**

Existing survey evidence can be supplemented by a more in-depth exploration of disparities and the reasons for them. This could be by way of a full-scale survey, focus group discussions (FGDs), or one-on-one interviews (see box 5.5).

BOX 5.5 **Obstacles to Finance in South Africa**

5

IFC undertook a study in **South Africa** to explore why women, particularly black women (more than 90 percent of whom run their own businesses), find it difficult to access finance. The study was based on (i) existing survey evidence, (ii) focus group discussions with businesswomen, and (iii) interviews with financial institutions. Key obstacles to women accessing finance were found to include

- lack of collateral;
- financial literacy: poor understanding of financial terminology and law;
- attitudes of banks (only one of South Africa's four major banks was contemplating a specific program to increase its share of female-owned enterprises);
- lack of awareness of availability of finance (few women in business know about the different institutions, their products, or how to access them—out of 170 women surveyed in four provinces, only seven were familiar with the offerings for small and medium enterprise finance from financial institutions in their province); and
- lack of financial confidence: women are more risk averse than men.

Source: Access to finance for women entrepreneurs in South Africa: challenges and opportunities, IFC 2005.

Evidence may emerge of discriminatory attitudes and treatment of women on the part of financial institutions:

When I asked the bank for a loan, they asked me where my husband was.

— Woman entrepreneur, Kenya

Discussions may be held with men and women who have successfully financed their businesses through secured lending and those who have been unable to do so. Candidates for interviews could be found through business associations (including women's business associations). Microfinance institutions may have successful (female) clients seeking to make the transition to the formal lending system, and their experiences may be relevant. Annex B contains a pro forma questionnaire suitable to be used as the basis for a survey, focus group discussion, or one-on-one interview.

> Although banking laws do not discriminate against women borrowers, banks in many countries in the **Middle East**[8] ask for the husband to be a cosigner—even if he lacks financial resources or is not involved in the woman's business. The intent is to ensure that the woman's activities do not interfere with the wishes of her family or her husband.

1.3 Analyze the Legal and Administrative Framework

Secured lending reform requires an understanding of the existing legal framework, in particular the extent to which it facilitates movable assets being used as collateral. Consideration should be given to the extent to which the legal framework enables women to own (and therefore use as collateral) movable assets and to whether the law discriminates in other ways against women when they seek to access finance (see box below for examples). Annex C contains a checklist of issues to consider.

> In **Cameroon,** married women have no property rights. The civil code states, "The husband alone administers matrimonial property . . . the husband shall administer all personal property of his wife" (articles 1421 and 1429).
>
> Until very recently in **Lesotho,** women were considered as minors and thus were ineligible to undertake legal transactions in their own right.

Local women lawyers' organizations (for example, the local branch of the international women lawyers' association, FIDA), or NGOs promoting women's rights are often well placed to provide assistance in analyzing these issues.

The country's international treaty obligations (see box) and any guarantees of equality contained in the constitution should be examined. If legal restrictions on women's property rights or ability to participate in secured lending conflict with these overarching obligations, the case for reform may be stronger.

BOX 5.6 **International Commitments on Women's Access to Finance**

The Convention on the Elimination of All Forms of Discrimination Against Women (CEDAW) requires states to ensure that women have equal rights to obtain bank loans, mortgages, and other forms of credit.

The Beijing Platform for Action commits to providing women with access to finance and credit and eliminating biases against women in finance laws.

The Protocol to the African Charter on Human and People's Rights on the Rights of Women in Africa commits states to create conditions to promote and support the occupations and economic activities of women.

5

Step 2   Solution Design

The diagnostic undertaken in step 1 will reveal the particular barriers that women face when seeking secured lending. Step 2 provides possible solutions to address them. These are not "one-size-fits-all" solutions, but, rather, examples of approaches that will need to be adapted for particular contexts.

The diagnostic may reveal barriers that are beyond the scope of secured lending reform. For example, underlying social issues, such as intrahousehold relationships and allocation of resources, may affect women's willingness or ability to apply for loans. A secured lending program cannot address these issues directly, but it can mitigate these factors by providing an enabling legal, regulatory, and administrative environment.

Step 2.1 is the starting point for solution design: a clear determination and agreement of the impact the reforms seek to achieve in relation to gender.

2.1   Agree on Gender-Related Program Results

The starting point for solution design is to be clear about what the planned package of reforms aims to achieve for women. It may be helpful to formulate these goals in discussion with women entrepreneurs and women's business associations. The key desired outcome is likely to be an increase in the amount of secured lending to female-owned businesses, in terms of the numbers of women receiving loans as well as the value of the loans.

2.2   Undertake Legal and Regulatory Reform to Enable and Encourage Lending to Women

If the diagnostic (see annex B) reveals discriminatory laws relating to banking, lending or property rights, these provisions should be repealed. In addition, proactive legal reform should be considered as a method to enhance women's ability to access secured lending. This may include amending the regulatory framework for credit reference agencies to enable women to establish their own credit history, separate from their husbands'. Reform to prohibit gender discrimination in relation to credit applications may also improve women's access to secured lending (see box 5.7). If this course is taken, careful consideration should be given to a realistic and sustainable enforcement mechanism.

Developing partnerships with organizations already providing credit to women may facilitate reform.

> **BOX 5.7** **Examples of Nondiscriminatory Acts on Finance**
>
> Many countries' constitutions (or other overarching laws) outlaw discrimination on the grounds of gender. But such provisions may not apply to private transactions (such as banking). If this is the case, consideration should be given to extending nondiscrimination provisions so that they apply in the private sphere:
> - The **UK** Sex Discrimination Act, 1975 (as amended) prohibits gender discrimination in private transactions to supply goods, facilities, and services, including credit.
> - The **USA** Equal Credit Opportunity Act 1974 prohibits discrimination on the grounds of gender (or race) in relation to credit applications. It was extended by the Women's Business Act 1988 to include business loans.

2.3 Undertake Awareness Raising Directed at Women

If the diagnostic revealed that women have limited knowledge of or access to information about accessing finance for their businesses, a program of awareness raising may be necessary. This could include financial literacy schemes and education for women on the benefits of accessing finance.

Possible partners for these types of initiatives include

- commercial banks (see box on Access Bank in Nigeria);
- institutions involved in administering the new secured lending regime;
- institutions familiar with lending to women—even if in a different context— such as microfinance institutions; and
- women's business associations.

2.4 Undertake Capacity Building for Financial Institutions and Implementers of New Laws

The diagnostic may reveal a lack of familiarity on the part of financial institutions with the female market segment. Regulatory and other institutions involved in implementing, monitoring, and evaluating the new regime may similarly not be attuned to gender issues, so capacity building in relation to gender issues with these institutions may be appropriate. Key issues to cover in such capacity building are listed in annex D. International experience may be drawn upon (see box 5.8).

5

BOX 5.8 **Global Banking Alliance for Women**

In 2000, four banks that had been recognized by the Organisation for Economic Co-operation and Development as "best practice" banks in reaching the women's market in their countries formed a consortium called the *Global Banking Alliance for Women*. Member banks collaborate on identifying and sharing global best practices in financial service delivery to women. Initially started by banks from Australia, Canada, New Zealand, the United Kingdom, and the United States, the alliance now has 22 members, including members from Africa, the Middle East, and Latin America.[9]

5

Step 3   Implementation and M&E

The general points on implementation and monitoring and evaluation in the core module should be applied to secured lending reform programs. In addition, the following points should be considered in relation to M&E.

3.1   Ensure Key Information Can Be Gender Disaggregated

Although potentially challenging, it is vital to ensure that key data can be gender disaggregated so that the impact of reforms on women can be monitored and evaluated. The central bank and commercial lending institutions may not gather gender-disaggregated statistics on lending patterns. And it may be difficult with loans to determine whether a family business is owned by the husband or wife (see box 2.3 of module 2 on definition of female-headed businesses) or both.

Despite possible difficulties, to the extent possible without imposing undue costs, data should be gender disaggregated. At the minimum it will be important to gather information about levels of lending to women following the institution of reforms. Discussions should be held with the central bank, with new institutions administering the new regime (such as movable property registries), and with commercial lending institutions to develop a suitable system. Institutions already focusing on lending to women may have useful knowledge to share about gender-disaggregated data collection systems.

3.2   Incorporate Output and Outcome Indicators That Highlight Gender Aspects of the Program

5

Gender issues should be incorporated within the program's M&E framework at the output and outcome levels. Table 5.1 provides a template for incorporating gender in indicators typically used in secured lending reform programs.

Table 5.1: M&E Indicators

Indicator/Data required	Gender focus (Gender-disaggregation)	Source of data
Output indicators		
• Number of operational manuals produced • Training and outreach	• Qualitative indicator: gender-inclusive focus (customer service); gender issues articulated and addressed • Core indicator: number and/or percentage of men and women participating or benefiting	• Manuals produced • Agency management • FGDs • Interviews with business-women

(Continued)

Table 5.1: M&E Indicators (*Continued*)

Indicator/Data required	Gender focus (Gender-disaggregation)	Source of data
• Workshops and outreach events to disseminate the new secured transactions reform and registry	• Gender disaggregate the data on participants	• FGDs • Agency management • Women's business associations • Sample surveys

Outcome indicators

Indicator/Data required	Gender focus (Gender-disaggregation)	Source of data
• Changes in laws, regulations and procedures that discriminate against women	• Do women have to obtain husband or other male permission to engage in business transactions (including opening a bank account or securing a loan)?	• FGDs • Women's business associations • Women's legal rights • NGOs • Country legal and social analysis
• Average number of days to file a security interest	• Number of days disaggregated by gender of business owner	• Tracking survey • Agency management • Regulatory Impact Assessmen Survey • FGDs • Women's businesses and associations
• Average official cost to file a security interest	• Cost disaggregated by gender of business owner (to capture corruption or other differences) • Corruption incidence disaggregated by gender of business owner	• Tracking survey • Agency management • Regulatory Impact Assessment Survey • FGDs • Women's businesses and associations
• Movable property registry established or became operational	• Percentage of filings of borrower	• Agency management • FGDs • Women's businesses and associations
• Improved user perceptions of services provided	• Disaggregate by gender	• Agency management • Regulatory Impact Assessment Survey • FGDs • Women's businesses and associations

5

Annex A Checklist of Questions for Commercial Bank and Lending Institution Owners

Note: Precise gender-disaggregated statistics are unlikely to be available and are not necessary. Estimates will suffice.

1. What types of secured lending does your institution provide (for example, mortgages, leasing, pledges)?
2. What percentage of your institution's lending requires collateral?
3. In relation to your secured lending portfolio:
   - What percent has land as collateral and what percent is secured by movable assets?
   - What percent lending to women has land as collateral and what percent is secured by movable assets?
   - What percent lending to men has land as collateral and what percent is secured by movable assets?
4. Of the people who apply to you for loans, what is the proportion of women to men?
5. Of (i) female applicants and (ii) male applicants, what percent are successful in their loan applications?
6. What repayment rates are achieved by (i) male borrowers and (ii) female borrowers?
7. What are your views on why (if it is the case) your institution lends less often to women than to men, for example:
   - Women tend to be less financially literate than men.
   - Women tend to be more risk averse than men.
   - Women do not have the required collateral.
   - Women tend to be more likely to default.
   - Women do not have bankable projects.
   - Women do not apply for loans.
8. How do you outreach to potential new loan customers? Does any of your outreach specifically target women?

5

Annex B   Sample Questionnaire for Business Owners

Introduction

1. Type of business: legal form (incorporated, partnership, sole trader, other)
2. Sector or main product
3. Size (number of employees and turnover)
4. Gender of owner(s)
5. Gender of manager(s)

Note: The questions that follow will need to be used flexibly, taking into account the context and level of knowledge and experience of interviewees. Approaches should vary depending on whether the questions are being used in the context of a survey, focus group discussion, or one-on-one interview.

Access to Secured Lending

1. Where would you go if you wanted to obtain finance for your business; what sources of finance are open to you?
2. Have you ever tried to obtain funds for your business?
3. If you have tried to obtain funds for your business—
   - Where from?
   - Were you successful?
   - Did you have to give collateral for the loan? If so, of what type?
   - Did you have collateral of the type they wanted?
   - Do you feel you suffered poor treatment as a result of your gender (for example, the bank preferred to deal with your spouse or you experienced some form of sexual harassment)?
4. Does your business have any assets for example—
   - Stock
   - Machinery
   - Equipment
   - Vehicle
   - Book debts
5. If your business does have such assets, would you be prepared to use them as security for a loan?
6. Have you encountered gender discrimination when you have sought finance for your business?
7. Do you think your gender makes it more or less difficult to access finance? Why?

5

Annex C   Legal Checklist

Note: In each case, identify legal basis (name and date of law or regulation) for answer.

General

1. Can women enter into secured transactions in the same way as men? For example—
   - Are women regarded as legal minors in contract law?
   - Is the age of majority the same for women as for men?
   - Is a man's consent or signature needed for a woman to apply for credit?
   - Are there any legal provisions specifically relating to usury and women? If so, what are they?
2. Is there a constitutional or other legal prohibition on gender discrimination? If so, does it apply to private transactions, such as with lending institutions?

Women's Property Rights

3. Do women (including married women) have the same legal right as men to own property in their names?
4. Do women (including married women) have the same legal right as men to use their personal property as security for a loan? Are there any additional requirements, for example, to obtain the consent of the husband or a male relative?
5. What are women's rights to matrimonial property on the death of their husbands or in the event of divorce?
6. If women have the legal right to own property, does the formal law provide for this to be overridden in any circumstance, for example, by application of customary law?

Ability of Women to Register Secured Transactions

If there is a registry for registering some or all types of secured transactions—
7. Is the registration process the same for women (including those who are married) as for men? For example, do women have to file additional documents, answer additional questions, go to a different place, or go through additional procedures?
8. Are women permitted to undertake the registration process without involving men (for example, to accompany them to the registration office)?

5

9. If personal attendance at the office is necessary, are there any travel restrictions for women?

Note: The existing registry (if one exists) should be asked to give its perspective on questions 7–9.

Ability of Women to Establish Independent Credit History

10. If there are laws on credit information, do they treat women (including married, divorced, and separated women) in the same way as men?

If there is an operational credit reference agency[10]—

11. Does the agency collect information on the gender of the individuals covered?
12. Is credit history established through participation in microfinance or are group lending schemes captured by the registry?
13. To what extent are a married person's assets considered to be consolidated with his or her spouse's assets for the purposes of the credit history? Is the situation the same for men and women? If polygamy is common, how does that affect the answer?
14. Is it usual for both the husband's and the wife's name to appear on documents used to establish credit history, for example, utility bills? If no, which name is more likely to appear, the husband's or the wife's?

Note: A credit reference agency (if one exists) should be asked to give its perspective on questions 11–14.

5

Annex D   Capacity Building Checklist

For commercial lending institutions participating in a new secured transactions regime—

1. Benefits of targeting female-owned businesses
2. Methods for targeting female-owned businesses
3. Suitability of premises, opening hours, and so forth for women clients
4. Staff attitudes to women clients
5. Collection of gender-disaggregated data, for example, on lending, repayment rates

For central banks and organizations administering the new movable property regime, for example, movable property registry—

1. Benefits of enhancing women's participation in secured lending
2. Methods of awareness-raising among women in relation to the reformed system
3. Collection of gender-disaggregated data

5

Notes

1. See summary of evidence in World Bank, *Millennium Development Goals Global Monitoring Report* (World Bank, 2007), 110.
2. DFID, Briefing Note No. 5, *Gender and Growth*, 2007.
3. Leasing is frequently regarded as a form of secured lending, and is often regulated as such. Strictly speaking, however, title to the asset remains with the lending institution until full payment has been made.
4. Mark Pitt and Shahidur Khandker. "The Impact of Group-Based Credit Programs on Poor Households in Bangladesh: Does the Gender of Participants Matter?" *Journal of Political Economy* 106 (1998): 958–96.
5. It is highly unlikely to be skewed in favor of women.
6. That is, assets that are not land.
7. http://www.finscope.co.za/about.html.
8. Chamlou, 2008.
9. To read more about the Global Banking Alliance for Women, see http://www.gbaforwomen.org/.
10. A credit reference agency is an entity that collects credit information on individuals, which is then made available to lenders to determine the credit history of potential borrowers.

Alternative Dispute Resolution

This Module Should be Used in Conjunction with the Core Module

Alternative dispute resolution (ADR) aims to achieve efficient, inexpensive conflict resolution mechanisms for businesses in emerging economies. A typical ADR initiative might focus on (i) establishing a supportive legal framework for ADR, (ii) building support within the judicial system, (iii) raising awareness on the advantages of using ADR within the broader business community, and (iv) creating financially sustainable ADR centers.

This module can be used to introduce or strengthen alternative dispute resolution mechanisms for commercial disputes. It explores the extent to which women face difficulty when they seek to access commercial justice. It then considers the potential for commercial ADR to address any such difficulties and to ensure that women can access justice on an equal footing with their male counterparts. The module (i) provides tools to analyze the different experiences of men and women seeking commercial justice; to identify the gender specific barriers faced by women when their commercial rights are infringed; and to explore whether ADR could address some of these barriers (step 1 – diagnostic); (ii) provides solutions to address the gender issues and barriers revealed in the diagnostic in the context of programs to introduce or strengthen ADR (step 2 – solution design); and (iii) suggests ways to incorporate gender into the implementation and monitoring and evaluation of ADR programs (step 3).

For the purposes of this module, the primary focus is on commercial mediation, a key form of ADR for commercial disputes.

Summary

MODULE 6

Why Gender Matters

There is growing evidence[1] that restricted access to commercial justice can represent a significant barrier for women. Women's basic commercial rights (such as to own property) can be unclear and uncertain, for example, because of conflicts between formal and customary legal systems. In some cases women's right to own land or other property is explicitly denied, for example, by a constitution that gives priority to discriminatory customary law[2] or by a matrimonial code that makes a woman's property her husband's upon marriage.[3] (See fuller discussion in core module.) In addition, women can face barriers and discrimination when they seek to uphold their commercial rights through the courts.

In Egypt, it takes female-headed firms an average of 86 weeks to resolve disputes about overdue payments. This is eight months longer than the 54 weeks taken by male-headed firms to resolve these disputes.[4] Gender and Growth Assessments undertaken by IFC in Kenya, Tanzania, and Uganda point to the linkage between women's ability to access commercial justice and their ability to participate in economic activity.

If women have limited commercial and property rights and are hampered by lack of enforcement by authorities, their individual businesses and, ultimately, the economy as a whole suffers. Business transactions are constrained and assets are inefficiently employed. Evidence shows that an enabling legal environment for women is necessary, albeit insufficient, for improvements in women's economic empowerment. Significant correlation exists between a women's legal empowerment index[5] and the gender empowerment measure, the latter reflecting the level of women's economic decision making, share of income, and political representation.

The development of ADR helps to realize an individual's right to access to justice and transparency. Therefore, any ADR program should not perpetuate

6

| **BOX 6.1** | **Women's Challenges in Accessing Justice** |

The **Kenya** GGA[6] notes frequent misunderstanding and misinterpretation in the court system—particularly by the lower courts—of women's property and inheritance rights.

The **Tanzania** GGA[7] highlights the challenges women face when they seek to enforce their property rights. For example, a woman's business assets can be summarily confiscated by the police on the breakdown of the marriage and handed over to her estranged husband.

The **Uganda** GGA[8] highlights the dominance in justice delivery agencies of men and the prevalence of patriarchal values and insensitivity to gender issues.

the existence of gender inequities nor be structured so as to create gender inequities. There should be no systemic barriers to any individual's participation in the ADR program. A by-product of ADR programs is the creation of employment and elevation of a practitioner's status. ADR programs can also have the beneficial effect of creating employment for and raising the status of female lawyers. In both developed and developing countries, many mediators are women. Particularly in environments where the legal profession is male dominated, or where women are barred from judicial office, mediation can offer viable job alternatives to female lawyers and give them valuable professional experience.

6

Step 1 Diagnostics

Step 1 aims to ascertain (i) whether there are differences in the types of commercial disputes encountered by women and men; (ii) whether women and men make equal use of the existing commercial justice system; (iii) whether there are gender specific barriers to accessing the existing system; and (iv) the extent to which the new or strengthened ADR mechanism could address the problems identified.

> The critical steps to be taken during an initial project design phase (in the absence of a full diagnostic at that point) are identified by a magnifying glass icon. 🔍

1.1 Obtain Gender-Disaggregated Private Sector Views on the Commercial Justice System

The starting point for addressing issues related to commercial justice is to seek the views and experience of the private sector—of both men and women. Where different approaches are considered for the introduction of ADR in emerging markets, assessing gender inequities in access to justice will help to ensure that ADR models do not perpetuate such inequities. A thorough examination of the legislative framework and cultural norms in terms of dispute resolution will be required in this regard.

Existing survey evidence (for example, commercial justice baseline studies or studies produced by legal sector reform programs) can provide useful gender-disaggregated data on commercial justice issues and, in particular, on the nature and severity of barriers to accessing the commercial justice system. If the surveys are recent, and the data published in them are not gender disaggregated, it may be possible to obtain the raw data from the survey organization for further analysis.

Even if existing gender-disaggregated data exist, a more in-depth exploration of gender issues may still be required during a full diagnostic. Annex A contains a pro forma questionnaire for business owners designed to determine if there are (i) gender differences in the level and scope of commercial disputes encountered, (ii) barriers to accessing the dispute resolution system, (iii) perceptions of the system, and (iv) views on the appropriateness of ADR to deal with commercial issues. The questions may be used in the context of one-on-one interviews, focus group discussions (FGDs), or more formal surveys. The questions should be asked of both male and female business owners to enable comparison. Some of the questions explore the experiences of men and women who have firsthand knowledge of the commercial justice or ADR system. Suggestions for clients who could answer these questions may be obtained from local legal practitioners.

6

1.2 Interview Legal Stakeholders with Gender Expertise

Lawyers with firsthand experience and understanding of the commercial justice system should be consulted. As well as commercial judges and lawyers, the views of lawyers with insights into gender issues may be particularly valuable, for example, women judges or magistrates associations, women's lawyers associations, and nongovernmental organizations (NGOs) providing legal advice and assistance to women. Issues that should be explored include

- the extent to which the legal profession is male dominated and whether this presents barriers to women bringing cases (percentage of female judges and lawyers);
- whether there are discriminatory attitudes on the part of judges or the legal profession toward women in the context of commercial cases (see box);
- anecdotal evidence on the proportion of commercial cases brought by women; and
- views on ways to make the system more accessible to women.

Kenya

"We should not be forgetful of historical truths that the action of women on our destiny has been and is, unceasing: and that since the Great Fall in the Garden, woman has continued to baffle. We recall that through women's incitement, mankind was banished and doomed to die. . . ."

Kenya High Court 1995, *Beatrice Kimani v. Evanson Njoroge* HCCC no 1610/95

1.3 Consider the Legal Framework

Primary legislation, court rules, or the wider legal framework may contain legal impediments to women taking legal action. For example, women may be treated as legal minors, or their evidence may be considered to be worth less than a man's. Local lawyers with appropriate experience and women's lawyers associations may have ready access to information on these issues and should be consulted. A checklist of key issues is provided in annex B.[9]

1.4 Mine Court or ADR Records

Data should be obtained on male and female usage of the existing commercial justice system. Case-management systems and court registers may yield data on the proportion of cases brought by men and women, respectively. This needs to be considered against the proportion of male- to female-owned firms (see table 6.1).

Table 6.1: Hypothetical Analysis of Gender Balance of Potential Claimants

Type of court	Jurisdiction	Nature of typical business claimant	Percentage of female owners
High Court	Cases more than US$500	Large or medium-sized firms	5 percent
High Court Annexed Mediation	Cases more than US$500	Large or medium-sized firms	5 percent
Magistrates Court	Cases up to US$500	Small firms	50 percent

Source: Authors.

"Going to a commercial arbitrator is no different than going to court. Court fees and arbitration fees are both very high. And because the processes are so time consuming and have an impact on the business, enterprises don't have time to pursue them."

— Woman entrepreneur, Vietnam

Gender-disaggregated data on the outcome of cases (the percentage found in favor of female and male litigants) and on the time and cost of case processing should also be gathered, if they are available.

However, gathering such detailed information is likely to be challenging and may prove impossible. Case-management systems may not exist at all, particularly in lower courts. Even if they do exist, they may not record the gender of claimants. If this is the case, proxy data should be obtained, for example, by analyzing the court register for cases filed over a day or week or by analyzing the current caseload of a judge or magistrate.

6

An analysis of the High Court register in **Ghana** revealed that only a tiny minority of commercial cases are brought by women. Men are the dominant users.

Step 2   Solution Design

The diagnostic will reveal the extent to which women are users of the existing commercial justice system and the reasons for any exclusion from it they may face. Based on this analysis, step 2 describes how to address gender issues in the design of ADR programs.

It will not always be appropriate to address all gender inequalities related to commercial justice in the context of an ADR program. For example, women's unequal property rights or rights to land probably go beyond the reasonable scope of ADR—involving significant policy decisions, primary legislation, and possibly constitutional reform. However, an ADR program does have the potential to enhance women's ability to enforce the rights they have and to challenge discriminatory provisions and practices. In a mediation process the mediator is not bound to entertain only matters of right. Parties may explore underlying interests so women may be able to achieve outcomes that create contractual rights resulting from a mediation agreement that did not previously exist. This is another core argument for the adoption of ADR.

2.1   Agree on Gender-Related Program Results

The specific results the ADR program is seeking in relation to female-owned businesses should be identified up front, on the basis of the key issues identified in the diagnostic phase. The indicators are likely to reflect the effect that the introduction of ADR or the strengthening of existing ADR systems will have on women's access to and experience of commercial justice. Possible indicators may include

- improved satisfaction with the commercial justice system by businesswomen;
- increased proportion of female claimants in the commercial justice system; and
- increased proportion of female mediators in the ADR system.

2.2   Undertake Legal and Regulatory Reform to Abolish Discriminatory Provisions

The diagnostic may reveal specific provisions in the court rules, rules of evidence, or more general legal framework that have an impact on women's ability to apply for and obtain commercial justice on the same basis as their male counterparts. If this is the case, agreement should be sought to amend or repeal discriminatory provisions (see box).

> **The Supreme Court of Texas Gender Bias Task Force** found that gender-biased treatment toward litigants and counsel of both genders had a negative impact on the litigation process and could affect case outcome.[10] Subsequently, detailed guidelines were developed to address gender bias.

2.3   Provide an ADR Environment Conducive to Women

As with women interacting with public officials (see box in paragraph 2.5 of module 2), women may also be at a disadvantage in the courts. Indeed, the courts may offer scope for worse corruption and harassment, with repeated adjournments resulting in multiple interactions with court officials.

> Transparency International's Global Corruption Report 2007 notes that corruption in justice systems has a disproportionate effect on women, while acknowledging that the direct evidence is rather limited as corruption surveys have not been sufficiently gender disaggregated.

The diagnostic step may also reveal other ways in which women are disadvantaged when they seek to enforce their legal rights—for example, by sexist attitudes on the part of judges.

> Official investigations of corruption in **Tanzania** and **Kenya** found that sexual extortion of women—that is, seeking sexual favors in return for favorable decisions—was one aspect of corrupt practice in the justice systems.[11]

ADR programs should be designed to address these issues. Possible solutions include the following:

- Ensure gender balance in ADR staff. For example, in Rwanda, there is a legal requirement that women should comprise a minimum of 30 percent of the membership of community mediation committees.[12] Evidence suggests that increased female representation tends to make courts more accessible to women.[13] Women may prefer to interact with women and men with men (see box).

  However, mediation services and training generally tend to target former judges and litigators as potential mediators—a group that is usually male-dominated. The pool may need to be widened if a gender balance is to be achieved.

6

> **Uganda**'s ADR Centre (CADER) is colocated with the Commercial Court and has obtained most of its business through cases referred to it by the court. Most of CADER's mediators are women. CADER reports that this has led to resistance to mediation from many men in the business community. Resistance may also reflect the fact that the mediators tended to be young and had limited experience.[14]

- Provide gender-specific training for ADR providers. This should ensure sensitivity to gender issues, particularly the perceived power imbalances between genders, and also ensure that the ADR provider is knowledgeable about cultural values and norms of both genders in the local context.

A skilled mediator should ensure that the power differences between men and women that put women at a "disadvantage" in negotiating with men are not brought into play. Mediation validates the parties' ability to speak for themselves by the mediator's use of specific skills that help parties explore options and the possible repercussions of different courses of behavior or action. But if handled incorrectly, mediation can silence the voices of women and result in unfair settlements that fail to address their needs.

• Provide an environment in which women feel free to speak.

Traditionally in **Rwanda**, women are not encouraged to speak in public. This is exemplified by the saying that "no hen cries in the presence of the rooster."[15]

• Provide separate front office desks, waiting areas, and bathroom facilities for women.
• Consider whether opening hours are convenient for women (who may have to juggle their business responsibilities and domestic duties). Also consider child care issues (see box 6.2).
• Ensure that operational and procedural manuals, codes of conduct, customer charters, and so forth, address gender issues and set out the level of service that women should expect.

6

BOX 6.2   Good Practice Examples

The courthouse in Chikako, **Malawi**, recently installed a latrine. Before this, justice was a strictly male affair, and women rarely traveled to the courthouse. Modest Malawian women did not feel comfortable using the bush to relieve themselves with so many men around. The result of the new latrine can be seen in a recent case to determine rival claims to the post of chief. A crowd of more than 300 people came to the court to listen to the case—half men and half women.

In the **United States**, some cities, such as New York and Washington, DC, provide free or subsidized day care services close to court premises to enable mothers to attend court and facilitate access to justice.

Source: The Times newspaper 2008, UNIFEM 2008–009.

- Grievance mechanisms, complaints boxes, and help desks should be undertaken by teams that include women.
- Include women's business associations on ADR program user or oversight committee. Also involve local women's interest groups in design and implementation to ensure compliance with international best practice and human rights obligations in relation to gender.

2.4   Develop Outreach Activities or Communications Strategy

The new or strengthened ADR system should be actively promoted to businesswomen. Strategies for doing so could include

- engaging with women's business organizations and NGOs supporting women entrepreneurs;
- developing an advertising campaign about commercial justice in general and ADR in particular aimed specifically at women entrepreneurs (radio may be a particularly effective medium as women may have lower literacy rates than men); and
- developing user guides to commercial justice and ADR systems aimed specifically at women entrepreneurs (bearing in mind that women may have lower literacy rates than men).

2.5   Ensure ADR Jurisdiction Addresses Commercial Disputes Encountered by Women

The diagnostic in step 1 may reveal that women tend to encounter particular types of commercial disputes, such as over property rights. If this is the case, these types of cases should be included within the auspices of the ADR program's jurisdiction.

6

Step 3   Implementation and M&E

The general point on implementation and monitoring and evaluation in the core module should be applied to ADR programs. In addition, the following issues should be considered in relation to M&E.

3.1   Put in Place Systems to Gather Gender-Disaggregated Data within an ADR Program

The ADR program's case management or M&E system should be designed to gather basic gender-disaggregated data so as to assess the impact of the program on women's access to commercial justice. At a minimum this will involve ensuring that the gender of the parties using the ADR system is recorded. (Further inquires will be needed where cases are brought in the name of a business rather than in the name of an individual.)

If possible, systems should also be put in place to gather gender-disaggregated data on the types of cases being referred to ADR and the level of satisfaction of users with the system.

3.2   Incorporate Output and Outcome Indicators That Highlight Gender Aspects of the Program

Output and outcome level ADR program indicators should also incorporate gender. Examples are provided in table 6.2.

Table 6.2: M&E Indicators

Indicator/Data required	Gender focus (Gender-disaggregation)	Source of data
Output indicators		
• Number of operational manuals produced • Training and outreach	• Qualitative indicator: gender-inclusive focus; gender issues articulated and addressed • Core indicator: number and/or percentage of men and women participating or benefiting	• Manuals produced • Agency management • FGDs • Interviews with businesswomen
Outcome indicators		
Number and percentage of cases successfully settled through ADR	• Disaggregate by gender of claimant	• ADR records

(Continued)

6

Indicator/Data required	Gender focus (Gender-disaggregation)	Source of data
Average number of days to settle a case through ADR	• Disaggregate by gender of claimant	• ADR records
Average official cost to settle a case through ADR	• Disaggregate by gender of claimant	• ADR records
Number of qualified mediators	• Percentage of male and female mediators • Differences in ways male and female mediators are used	• FGDs • Agency management

Annex A   Sample Questionnaire for Business Owners

Introduction

1. Size of business (number of employees/turnover)
2. Gender of owner(s)
3. Gender of manager(s)

Note: The questions below will need to be used flexibly, taking into account the context and level of knowledge and experience of interviewees. Approaches should vary depending on whether the questions are being used in the context of a survey, focus group discussion, or one-on-one interview. The concept of ADR may require explanation.

Commercial Justice System

Questions on Experience of the Commercial Justice System

1. Has your business been involved in a dispute in the past five years?
IF THE ANSWER TO QUESTION 1 IS YES, PLEASE ANSWER QUESTIONS 2 THROUGH 9.
2. If yes, what was the nature of the dispute? Was it concerning—
   - Property rights
   - Land
   - A debt
   - Employment
   - Other (please specify)

   Please give brief details.
3. Did the case go to court?
4. If not, how was it resolved?
5. How long did it take to finalize your case?
6. How much did it cost to finalize your case?
7. Were you asked for a bribe at any stage? If so, did you give it, and if you did, what did you receive in return?
8. Were you subject to any sexual harassment?
9. How easy was it to enforce the judgment or settlement you obtained?

Questions on Dispute Resolution Methods

10. What is your preferred method of resolving your business disputes?
11. If you wanted to involve a third party to help you resolve the issue, who would you involve?

12. Would you take a business dispute to court or ADR?
13. If not, why not?

Questions on Perceptions of the Current System

Note: To be adapted depending on whether the country has introduced ADR or not.
14. Do you consider the current court or ADR system to be—
    - Too expensive
    - Too difficult
    - Too formal
    - Male dominated
    - Inconvenient in its hours of operation
    - Too far away
    - Too complex
    - Unfair
15. Would it be a problem for you if your business dispute went to court or ADR and the case was heard by a judge or ADR provider of the opposite gender to you?
16. Would it be a problem for you to stand up and speak to give evidence before a court or ADR body in order to sort out a business dispute?
17. Do you know where to go to obtain legal advice about a business dispute if you need it?
18. What improvements would you like to see in the courts or ADR system to make it easier for you to use it to sort out business disputes?
19. What is your perception of the current commercial court or ADR system?
    - Very relevant for my business
    - Somewhat relevant for my business
    - Not relevant at all for my business

6

Annex B   Legal Checklist

Making Contracts

1. Do men and women have the same ability to enter into legally binding contracts (for example, is the age of full legal capacity the same for men as for women; do women need to obtain permission from their husbands or male relative)?

Enforcing Contracts

2. Do the laws and regulations relating to commercial litigation include any provisions that specifically apply to women?
3. Can women bring court proceedings in the same way as men?
4. Do women need to get permission from their husbands or male relative to begin court proceedings or to enforce a contract?
5. Do court procedures for civil and commercial cases differ in any way depending on whether a man or woman is the plaintiff (for example, are women treated as legal minors in court proceedings)?
6. Is different evidential weight put on the testimony of men versus that of women in civil proceedings?
7. Are judgments in civil and commercial cases in favor of a woman enforced in the same way as judgments obtained by a man?

The Court System

8. Are women equally able to hold judicial office as men?

6

Notes

1. Ellis, A. et al., *Gender and Economic Growth in Tanzania: Creating Opportunities for Women* (World Bank, 2007); Ellis, A., et al., *Gender and Economic Growth in Kenya: Unleashing the Power of Women* (World Bank, 2007); Ellis, A., C. Manuel, M. Blackden, *Gender and Economic Growth in Uganda: Unleashing the Power of Women* (World Bank, 2006); World Bank, *Doing Business 2009*, 2008.

2. As in Kenya.

3. As in Cameroon.

4. Nadereh Chamlou, *The Environment for Women's Entrepreneurship in the Middle East and North Africa Region* (World Bank, 2008), 26.

5. Cueva's 2006 index, based on the Cinganelli-Richards scores on government commitment and capacity to enforce women's social, economic, and cultural rights with the addition of variables on international rights instruments.

6. A. Ellis. et al., *Gender and Economic Growth in Kenya—Unleashing the Power of Women* (World Bank, 2007).

7. A. Ellis. et al., *Gender and Economic Growth in Tanzania: Creating Opportunities for Women* (World Bank, 2007).

8. A. Ellis. et al., *Gender and Economic Growth in Uganda—Unleashing the Power of Women.* (World Bank, 2005).

9. Doing Business Gender Law Library may provide useful data.

10. Report of the Gender Bias Task Force, Supreme Court of Texas, 1994.

11. United Republic of Tanzania, "Report of the Commission on Corruption" ("The Warioba Report") (Dar-es-Salaam:1996); and Government of Kenya, "Report of the Integrity and Anti-Corruption Committee of the Judiciary of Kenya" (the "Ringera Report") (2003).

12. Organic Law No 31/2006 of 14/08/2006 on Organisation, Jurisdiction, Competence and Functioning of the Mediation Committee, Article 4.

13. UNIFEM, "Removing Gender Biases from Judicial Processes." http://www.unifem.org/gender_issues/voices_from_the_field/story.php?StoryID=612, cited in *Who Answers to Women? Progress of the World's Women 2008/2009* (UNIFEM, 2007).

14. A. Ellis. et al. *Gender and Economic Growth in Uganda—Unleashing the Power of Women.* (World Bank, 2005).

15. Report of the 2006 Women's Legal Rights Initiative Conference on the Role of Women's Legal Rights in the Family and in Rwandan Society.

6

Special Economic Zones

This Module Should be Used in Conjunction with the Core Module

Special economic zones (SEZs) have been defined as "geographically delimited areas administered by a single body, offering certain incentives (such as duty-free importing and streamlined customs procedures) to businesses that physically locate within the zone."[1] SEZs enable new approaches (for example, to customs or business entry) to be piloted in support of wider economic reforms frequently associated with the encouragement of foreign direct investment and export development. In addition, in infrastructure-poor environments, SEZs can provide fully serviced sites with purpose-built facilities for sale or lease.[2]

This module provides guidance on the creation of a legal, regulatory, and administrative environment for SEZs, which is cognizant of gender issues. It (i) provides tools to analyze how SEZs can have different impacts on women and on men (step 1 – diagnostic); (ii) suggests solutions to address the gender issues revealed in the diagnostic to ensure that the potential benefits of SEZs are equally available to women and to men (step 2 – solution design); and (iii) suggests ways to incorporate gender into the implementation and monitoring and evaluation of programs to support the establishment of SEZs (step 3).

Summary

MODULE 7

Why Gender Matters

...for Employees of Firms Locating in an SEZ

Concerns relating to gender and SEZs tend to have centered around women's employment conditions and rights. Worldwide, 60 percent to 70 percent of SEZ employees are women, who tend to be engaged in labor-intensive, assembly-orientated activities requiring manual dexterity, such as garments, textiles, and electrical and electronic goods production.[3] Concerns include the exploitation of women through low wage levels, lack of training or skill upgrading, and suppression of labor standards and core labor rights, including trade unionization.[4] A recent publication has summarized the position:

> There are continuing concerns regarding work conditions and social protection, including women's rights in some countries. Some headway has been made in respect to gender discrimination and gender-related barriers in zones, including equal pay, pregnancy, and child care. Mexican legislation, for example, now explicitly prohibits discrimination on the basis of pregnancy. But gender discrimination continues in some zones, especially in terms of unequal pay, inadequate rights during pregnancy, suitable working hours, and forced dismissals when women reach the fourth month of pregnancy.[5]

Despite concerns about employment conditions and rights, overall SEZs have been a very effective tool for generating jobs for women in the formal labor market (box 7.1).

BOX 7.1 Effectiveness of Special Economic Zones in Job Creation for Women

Kenya

The new and largest investments in **Kenya's** textile and clothing sector are taking place within its export processing zone (EPZ), introduced in 1990. Textiles are the dominant sector in the EPZs, accounting for more than 40 percent of firms, more than 90 percent of employment, and 70 percent of sales. Women account for more than three-quarters of workers in the sector and are often employed in low-skilled jobs, such as sewing and finishing. Most are young women, either recent school leavers who are using the work to provide income before continuing with their education, or single mothers. Men employed in the sector are generally older and act as supervisors.

(Continued)

7

BOX 7.1 Effectiveness of Special Economic Zones in Job Creation for Women (*Continued*)

Although the textiles and spinning sector pays the lowest wages in Kenya's EPZ, wages paid are similar to those in the informal sector and must comply with minimum wage laws. The current wage structure is up to 25 percent above the minimum wage.[6]

Bangladesh
The first EPZ in **Bangladesh** was established in Chittagong in 1983. Today there are eight EPZs in the country. This sector employs more than 200,000 workers, of which roughly 64 percent are women.[7] The bulk of jobs in the EPZ sector are in the garment and textile industries. EPZ firms are 5 percent of those producing garments and related goods, with the remainder locally owned private companies.[8] Nationally, the industry employs about 1.5 million workers, the majority of whom are women, but the concentration of women production workers in EPZs is higher than in domestically owned firms. Women employees are 75 percent of workers in fully foreign-owned garment firms compared with slightly less than 50 percent in locally owned garment firms and about 40 percent in all manufacturing firms in 1998.[9]

Although women have a large share of the jobs in garment EPZs, they are concentrated in lower-paid production jobs, with men dominating in supervisory and skilled positions. For example, only 35 percent of workers in the knitwear industry, which is more technology intensive than the woven garment industry, are women.[10] This is consistent with other parts of the world in which women tend to be overlooked as workers as industries move up the technology ladder to more skilled and capital-intensive production.

Nevertheless, women in EPZs earn higher wages and enjoy better work conditions than those employed in locally owned firms. This is the result of several factors. Women employed in EPZs tend to have higher levels of education (on average eight years compared with four years in non-EPZ firms).[11] Also, EPZ factories produce higher-value items than locally owned firms, in large part a result of direct contact with retailers and fashion houses. Ongoing relationships with buyers and designers have expanded knowledge of the market, allowing EPZ firms to gain access to higher ends of the market.

Sources: Ellis et al. 2007; BEPZA 2008; Kabeer and Mahmud 2004; Bhattacharya 1998; and Chaudhuri-Zohir 2000.

7

Providing an environment in which women have successfully entered the formal labor market is an important achievement for SEZs. Cultural attitudes and norms that lead to lower educational attainment and expectations, direct discrimination in the workplace, informal discrimination through social networks, and time poverty have typically resulted in very limited female penetration of formal labor markets in developing countries. Worldwide, women are three times more likely than men to be found in the informal economy.[12] There is emerging evidence that this has, in turn, had significant impact on economic growth (see box 7.2).

But formal labor market employment opportunities for women in SEZs may be declining. As firms in SEZs begin to move away from simple assembly operations, women's access to these jobs is constrained. For example, in Malaysia, only 40 percent of the workers in SEZs are now female, down from 60 percent two decades ago.[13] Moreover, SEZs can sometimes enhance the informalization of women's work. For example, firms in Latin American and Asian EPZs are increasingly outsourcing to home-based women workers.[14]

…for Entrepreneurs

Women should have the same opportunities as men to set up businesses in SEZs. As far as local investors are concerned, SEZs present an opportunity to address the specific issues faced by female-headed firms that are discussed in this guide. In particular, women's highly restricted access to titled land is frequently cited as a critical constraint to their ability to start and grow a business. Through the provision of serviced sites, SEZs have the potential to make land available to women. In addition, if SEZ development is coupled with other measures to improve the business-enabling environment—for example, streamlined import and export procedures—this is an

---

BOX 7.2 **Impact of Women's Increased Labor Force Participation**

In 2003 between 0.9 percent and 1.7 percent of the regional growth difference between the **East Asia and the Pacific** and the **Middle East and North Africa** regions can be accounted for by gender gaps in labor force participation and education.[15]

Research undertaken in **India** suggests that women's limited labor market participation can result in reduced labor productivity. Increasing the ratio of women employees increased output by as much as 50 percent. Increasing women's engagement in management also improved firm performance and innovation.[16]

Source: DFID 2007.

7

opportunity to pilot other solutions suggested in this guide designed to address the specific barriers faced by women.

The extract that follows from IFC's *SEZ Practitioners' Guide* provides a checklist of gender-related issues related to SEZ development. These issues are further developed in this module.

BOX 7.3   Can SEZs Empower Women?

A large share of the output of export-oriented SEZs is garments. The majority of garment workers are unskilled women. At early stages of economic development, even an unskilled formal sector job can substantially enhance household income and consumption. However, women are particularly vulnerable to becoming trapped in low skill and low wage work. SEZ regulators and operators can support women through initiatives such as the following:

- Supporting local women-owned enterprises through business linkages to SEZ tenants;
- Providing non-fiscal incentives to women-owned tenants to locate in the SEZ-e.g. the operator sets aside office space for women's startup;
- Linking women-owned tenants with foreign companies with a policy of buying from women-owned entities;
- Developing operator and tenant charters and standard operating procedures meeting minimum gender requirements, e.g. relating to worker housing, transport, HR policies, grievance procedures;
- Employing specialist gender advisors;
- Providing crèche, healthcare, banking services within the SEZ, as well as training programs to: (i) upgrade women's skills in a range of occupations; and (ii) provide basic entry-level skills to the female labor pool.

Source: Special Economic Zones Practitioner's Guide: With Application to Conflict-Affected Countries. 2009. IFC ICAS.

7

Step 1   Diagnostics

Step 1 aims to consider through a gender lens (i) the labor law framework for SEZs, (ii) the framework for land acquisition in SEZs, (iii) other regulatory issues to be addressed through SEZ development, and (iv) SEZ authority policies and practice.

> The critical steps to be taken during an initial project design phase (in the absence of a full diagnostic at that point) are identified by a magnifying glass icon. 🔍

1.1   Consider Labor Law and Practice in Relation to Female Employees

🔍 Governments set the legal framework for employment practices in SEZs, which may be the same as the general standards in the country or specialized for SEZs. Particularly in the case of older, state-run SEZs, standards for employment practices have tended to be lower than national standards. The applicable labor laws and regulations should be reviewed to ensure that they do not contain provisions that discriminate against women. Annex A contains a checklist of key issues.

A full diagnostic should be supplemented by research into how labor standards are enforced in practice. Sources could include

- existing reports on labor standards, for example, ILO reports, reports of employees associations or trade unions, and reports of international or local NGOs; and
- interviews with employees, particularly those who have attempted to enforce their employment rights. Local employment lawyers may be able to identify relevant individuals. Annex B contains a pro forma questionnaire designed to be used as the basis for one-to-one interviews, focus group discussions (FGDs), or surveys. The questions should be asked of both male and female employees to enable comparisons to be made. International experience suggests that wage rates are likely to be a key issue (see box).

> Throughout **South Asia,** women's wages range from half to two-thirds of those received by men, even after controlling for educational attainment.[17]
>
> In **India,** the gender wage gap is growing and persists even among educated women and men.[18]
>
> In the **United Kingdom,** women's hourly pay was 17.1 percent less than men's pay.[19]

As background to this analysis, National Labour Force Surveys could be considered, which can be excellent sources for gender-disaggregated data on the labor market—for example, on the types of work undertaken by men and women (sector, full- or part-time, wage levels).

7

1.2 Consider Procedures for Acquiring Land Rights

SEZ development is frequently associated with the provision of serviced sites. In association with this, improved land use and land rights acquisition laws and regulations may be developed. The resulting arrangements for investors to acquire land in SEZs by purchase or lease should be reviewed through a gender lens. Annex A contains a checklist designed to ensure that the legal framework for land acquisition enables women business owners to acquire and develop SEZ land on the same basis as their male counterparts.

In addition, limited access to finance can be a major impediment for women seeking to purchase land.

1.3 Consider Other Regulatory Issues to Be Addressed through SEZ Development

Where SEZ development is designed to include piloting of improved approaches to wider investment climate issues—such as business entry, tax, or import or export procedures—the relevant sections of this *Practitioners' Guide* should be applied and diagnostics undertaken to highlight the gender issues involved.

1.4 Consider the Policies and Practices of the Authority Administering the SEZ

Modern best practice is for SEZs to be developed and administered by private sector rather than public bodies. Even when laws and regulations are gender neutral, attitudes and practices of such bodies (whether public or private) can discriminate against women.

Annex Ĉ contains a brief institutional gender equality checklist for SEZ authorities, to assess the extent to which their policies and practices facilitate cultivation of both female and male business owners. Where the SEZ authority is not yet in existence, the checklist should be discussed with the government body or ministry responsible for taking forward SEZ development.

7

Step 2   Solution Design

The diagnostic will reveal the extent to which the legal framework, policies, practices, and administrative arrangements for SEZs are appropriate for women as well as men. Step 2 sets out possible solutions to address the issues revealed in step 1. The solutions relate to women both as employees (step 2.2) and as business owners (steps 2.3–2.5). But step 2.1 is the starting point for solution design and flows directly from the diagnostic key stakeholders need to determine the intended development impact of SEZs on female employees and entrepreneurs.

2.1   Agree on Gender-Related Program Results

Government, the SEZ authority, and other stakeholders involved in SEZ development should be clear about what SEZs are intended to achieve as far as gender is concerned. Specific, measurable results should be identified in relation to the issues revealed in the diagnostic. If possible, these should be discussed and agreed upon by groups representing businesswomen and employees, and steps should be taken to include these groups in SEZ policy development. Possible indicators may include

- compliance with International Labour Organization (ILO) labor standards in relation to women employees, including maternity rights and equal pay for equal work;
- percentage of women employed in SEZs (and what percent occupy skilled posts); and
- percentage of female-owned businesses located in SEZs.

2.2   Ensure Best Practice Employment Legal and Regulatory Framework and Practice

Issues revealed in the diagnostic in relation to employment law and practice should be addressed. These may include the following:

- **Legal and regulatory reform**: EPZ law or the national employment code must ensure equal protection to female and male employees and address areas of potential discrimination (see checklist in annex A). Key issues are likely to include maternity benefits and equal pay, which may need careful consideration in light of international evidence (box 7.4).[20] Reform may be linked to trade agreements. For example, the Dominican Republic-Central America-United States Free Trade Agreement (CAFTA-DR) includes specific provisions on labor law reform.[21]

7

BOX 7.4 **Consequences of Maternity Leave and Pay**

Maternity leave and pay: Laws giving women maternity rights can have unintended adverse consequences:

(i) pricing women out of the formal labor market (although this is less likely where employment is gender segregated, since male workers are less likely to be substituted for female);

(ii) reducing female wage rates because (i) employers may factor maternity leave costs into their wage offer, and (ii) women who find maternity leave valuable may increase the supply of their labor, further contributing to a decline in female wages.

Where governments rather than employers bear the cost of maternity pay, these negative impacts are likely to be less.

- In **Uganda,** research has shown that well-intentioned labor reform to provide two months maternity leave (one month paid) would have been prohibitive for many smaller employers and would have discouraged them from hiring women of child bearing age.[22]
- In **Costa Rica,** legislation facilitating enforcement of maternity leave laws coincided with a decline in women's wages. Despite this, employment did not fall, suggesting that women valued the benefit of maternity leave.[23]
- Research on the impact of new maternity benefits in **Taiwan** in the 1980s suggested that despite the resulting rise in the relative cost of employing women, women's employment increased following the reform. Paid maternity leave raised the probability that women would remain in the workforce, returning to their former employer after childbirth.[24]

Equal pay and the minimum wage: Legislation to regulate wages can also have unintended consequences:

- Evidence from **India** points to the strong relationship between high levels of female employment and low wages. States where the wage differential between men and women is the highest are among those with the highest growth levels in India.[25]
- Gender-blind minimum wage legislation can also yield different outcomes for men and women. Cross-country evidence shows that labor force participation rates drop more for women than men when the minimum wage rises. For example, in **South Africa**, studies have suggested that minimum wage legislation may result in significant job losses in vulnerable occupation categories, such as low-paid domestic workers (who are mainly female). On the other hand, two-thirds of the beneficiaries of the **United Kingdom**'s minimum wage legislation are

(Continued)

7

women, and the legislation is credited with reducing the male-female pay gap by nearly 5 percent. Similarly, in **Indonesia**, a doubling of the minimum wage in the 1990s led to an increase in real wages and only a very modest decline in employment.

- There is some evidence that wages and other working conditions can be improved without hurting job growth. *Better Factories Cambodia*, a trade-related labor standards agreement signed in 1999, linked expansion of **Cambodia**'s U.S. market access to improvements in labor standards. The program has helped to boost employment conditions without jeopardizing export growth.

Sources: Ellis 2006; van der Meulen Rodgers 1999; Zveglich 2003; DFID 2007; Martin 1996; and Berik and van der Meulen Rodgers 2008.

- **Institutional reform**: This ensures effective enforcement of labor standards, including through inspection and mechanisms for labor dispute resolution (see box). Where provision is made for alternative dispute resolution (ADR) to resolve labor disputes, the ADR section of this *Practitioners' Guide* should be applied. The institutional gender equality checklist in annex C should be applied to inspection authorities to ensure that they are competent to uphold women's employment rights.

In **Tanzania**, in the 18 months since its inception, the recently established Commission for Mediation and Arbitration has successfully resolved nearly 3,000 cases that would otherwise have gone through the longer and more costly formal labor court.[26]

- **Promotion of best practices**: SEZs present an opportunity to promote best practices in female employment. This may be linked with corporate social responsibility initiatives, such as the United Nations Global Impact's global corporate responsibility code of conduct.

7

Emerging evidence of the economic benefits of enhanced women's labor market participation means that it makes sense for governments to promote female employment—and SEZs present an opportunity to do this. Consideration could be given to the services provided on SEZ sites, including provision of child care facilities (see box). This could have wider benefits: a recent study in Kenya[27] showed that reducing the price of child care significantly increased mothers' wage employment and put more girls, particularly older girls, in school.

> The Alltex EPZ Limited plant in the EPZ at Athi River in **Kenya** has created employment for more than 2,000 Kenyans, more than 80 percent of whom are women. The facility is the only establishment in the EPZ and the region so far that has provided a day nursery for working mothers with infants. The plant, one of the largest textile factories in the zone, is a joint venture between the Industrial Promotion Services (an affiliate of the Aga Khan Fund for Economic Development) and the Global Readymade Garments Industry LLC (Qatar).[28]

2.3 Ensure Women Can Acquire Land Rights in SEZs on the Same Basis as Men

Any legal restrictions on the ability of women to purchase or lease land in SEZs, and to borrow money to do so, should be removed (see checklist in annex A). If access to finance for land purchase has been identified as a major constraint, consideration could be given to supporting market-based lending programs aimed specifically at women (see module 5).

2.4 Address Other Regulatory Issues through a Gender Lens

Where SEZ development is designed to include piloting of improved approaches to the business enabling environment—such as business entry, tax, or import and export procedures—the relevant sections of this *Practitioners' Guide* should be applied and the proposed solutions considered so that gender issues are fully incorporated in the program design.

2.5 Promote "Female-Friendly" SEZs

SEZs have the potential to provide a conducive environment for women to locate and develop their businesses. SEZs can address (on a pilot basis) the legal, regulatory, and administrative constraints addressed in this *Practitioners' Guide* that frequently put women at a disadvantage. Given the overall economic benefits of both enhanced women's employment and entrepreneurial activity, there is scope for promoting SEZs that specifically market themselves as "female friendly"—in terms of their legal and regulatory environment, access to resources that are frequently scarce for women (especially land and finance), and employment practices.

7

Step 3   Implementation and M&E

The general points on implementation and monitoring and evaluation in the core module should be applied to SEZs. In addition, the issues in the following paragraphs should be considered in relation to M&E.

3.1   Ensure Data on SEZ Performance Can Be Gender Disaggregated

The monitoring and evaluation system for SEZ performance should be developed so that the data it collects can be gender disaggregated. Data for which gender disaggregation is likely to be important include

- information about employment in SEZs: percentage of men and women employees, wage rates, skill levels, and development;
- ownership of firms locating in SEZs; and
- satisfaction levels with start-up in SEZ and ongoing service provision.

3.2   Incorporate Indicators that Highlight Gender Aspects of SEZ Development

Gender should also be incorporated in output- and outcome-level SEZ program indicators. Examples are provided in table 7.1.

Table 7.1: M&E Indicators

Indicator/Data required	Gender focus (Gender-disaggregation)	Source of data
Output indicators		
• Number of manuals Analyses • Diagnostics produced	• Qualitative indicator: gender-inclusive focus	• Manuals produced • Agency management • FGDs
• Workshops and outreach events	• Core indicator: number and/or percentage of men and women partici-pating or benefiting	• FGDs • Agency management • Women's business associations • Sample surveys

(Continued)

7

Table 7.1: M&E Indicators (*Continued*)

Indicator/Data required	Gender focus (Gender-disaggregation)	Source of data
Outcome indicators		
• Creation of SEZs accessible to women entrepreneurs (that is, terms and conditions of leasing premises, suitability, and standard of services and facilities provided)	• Disaggregate by gender to determine equal treatment in these areas	• SEZ management • FGDs • Women's businesses involved in the SEZ • Women's business associations
• SEZ law and policy drafted • SEZ became operational	• Gender-inclusive SEZ policy • Welcoming of women investors and employees	• SEZ policy documents and management • Women's businesses and associations
• SEZ employment policy established	• Number and/or percentage of men and women employed in SEZ • Change over baseline • Gender-responsiveness of terms and conditions of employment	• SEZ management • FGDs • Women's businesses involved in the SEZ • Women's business associations

7

Annex A   Legal and Policy Checklist

The critical steps to be taken during an initial project design phase (in the absence of a full diagnostic at that point) are identified by a magnifying glass icon. 🔍

Labor Law

International Treaty Obligations

1. Have international treaties relating to the employment of women been ratified, and do they apply in SEZs? (See box for summary of key provisions.)

- The Convention on the Elimination of All Forms of Discrimination Against Women requires governments to take appropriate steps in all fields to eliminate discrimination against women, including in employment (article 11).
- ILO Conventions relating to nondiscrimination in employment include the promotion of equal opportunity and treatment in employment (Convention 111), equal pay for equal work (Convention 111), maternity leave and benefits (Convention 183), part-time and home-based work (Conventions 175 and 177, respectively), and the provision of child care facilities (Convention 156).
- The 2005 World Summit Outcome reaffirmed commitments to promoting gender equality and empowerment by, among other things, promoting women's equal access to labor markets, sustainable employment, and adequate labor protection (paragraph 58(d)).

2. Do free trade agreements or bilateral investment treaties or agreements contain obligations in relation to labor law reform?

Codes of Conduct

1. Do international or national codes of conduct relating to corporate social responsibility apply?

National Labor Laws

(The assumption is that national labor laws apply in SEZs; if not, these questions should be asked of the relevant law that does apply.)

🔍 1. Are there legal provisions in place to address discrimination in the workplace, including on the grounds of gender, marital status, pregnancy, or family responsibilities?

🔍 2. Are there legal provisions to deal with sexual harassment in the workplace?

7

3. Is there minimum wage legislation? Does it differentiate between men and women or between different sectors?

4. Is there legal provision for equal pay for work of equal value?

5. Are there legal provisions that require allowances or salaries to be paid only to male workers or heads of households?

6. Is there a legal prohibition against dismissing a woman because she is pregnant?

7. Are there legal provisions in place to deal with maternity leave and pay? What is the length of such leave? Who meets the cost of any such paid leave?

8. Are there any legal provisions for additional benefits for mothers other than maternity leave (for example, provision of daycare or breast-feeding facilities for mothers)? If yes, how are these paid for?

9. Are there legal provisions that discriminate against women in the workplace, for example, a gender-specific working hour restriction or restrictions on working in certain sectors?

10. Are there priority rules that apply to redundancy based on gender?

11. Are there legal requirements for the provision of culturally appropriate facilities for male and female workers (for example, washrooms)?

12. Are any categories of workers excluded from employment laws, such as home-based workers?

13. Are there legal provisions in place establishing a minimum ceiling for representation by women in worker unions?

14. Do legally mandated retirement provisions exist and are mandatory retirement ages the same for men and women?

Land and Mortgage Law

1. Can women acquire, occupy, and manage land on the same terms as men? Are there any specific legal provisions in the constitution or any other laws conferring such powers over land on women, or are such powers recognized as a part of the regular law without the need for special provisions? Are there laws that forbid or prevent women from acquiring and occupying land in their name?

2. Is the process for acquiring land in the SEZ the same for a woman as for a man? For example, does a woman require the consent of a male relative, or does she need to produce any additional documents? Can a woman register title to land in her name and do so without the need for permission from a male relative?

3. As a matter of law or practice, are there any special rules or restrictions on women obtaining a mortgage to finance the development of land in an SEZ that do not apply to men? If so, what are they and are they grounded in law or a matter of practice by mortgagors?

4. Does marital status affect any of the answers given above? If so, how?

7

Annex B   Sample Questionnaire for Employees

Note: The questions below will need to be used flexibly, taking into account the context and level of knowledge and experience of interviewees. Approaches should vary depending on whether the questions are being used in the context of a survey, focus group discussion, or one-on-one interview.

Introduction

1. Gender of employee
2. Nature of employment (sector, job title)
3. Number of employees in business? Percentage male and female?

Employment Practices and Disputes

1. Have you ever suffered from sexual harassment in the workplace?
2. Are male and female employees treated in the same way by your employers? If not, please explain the differences. They may relate to, for example—
   - Pay
   - Hours worked
   - Working conditions
   - Marital status
   - Parental responsibilities
   - Facilities provided by the employer
   - Access to promotion and supervisory positions
   - Access to training opportunities
3. Do you know what to do should you have a dispute with your employers?
4. Have you ever had a dispute with your employers? If so, please explain what action you took and how it was resolved.
5. Do you receive any training to improve your skills?

7

Annex C   Institutional Gender Equality Checklist

For:
- authorities developing and administering SEZs
- authorities responsible for inspecting and implementing compliance with labor laws and regulations

1. Does the organization have a customer charter that includes reference to gender equality issues?
2. Does the organization have formal links with women's organizations (business associations, women's employees associations) for consultation and input to policy development, management, and operations?
3. Is the organization's staff trained to handle gender issues sensitively?
4. Are women employed in the organization, especially at levels where they interact with the public and at decision-making levels?
5. Are institutional systems in place to monitor gender-disaggregated results, and are these regularly reported on?
6. Is gender equality seen as an explicit goal of the organization?
7. Are gender equality perspectives evident in the institution's major policy and planning documents guiding the work of the institution?
8. Additional question for SEZ authorities: Are SEZ site vacancies advertised in locations and through media as likely to be accessed by women as by men?
9. Additional question for labor inspection authorities: Have your staff been trained in labor standards relating to women, for example, maternity rights, rights when pregnant, equal pay, and how to deal with cases of sexual harassment?

Notes

1. This definition includes free trade zones, export processing zones (EPZs), freeports, enterprise zones, and single-factory EPZs.

2. This summary is taken from FIAS, *Special Economic Zones: Performance, Lessons Learned, and Implications for Zone Development*, 12.

3. Ibid.

4. For example, by the International Labour Organization, 1998, *Labour and Social Issues Relating to Export Processing Zones*, Geneva.

5. FIAS, *Special Economic Zones: Performance, Lessons Learned, and Implications for Zone Development*.

6. Ellis et al., *Gender and Economic Growth in Kenya*, 81.

7. Bangladesh Export Processing Zone Authority (BEPZA), "Export Processing Zones (EPZs) in Bangladesh: An Attractive Investment Destination," 3.

8. Kabeer and Mahmud, "Chains of Fortune: Linking Women Producers and Workers with Global Markets," 134–62.

9. Bhattacharya, "Export Processing Zones in Bangladesh: Economic Impact and Social Issues" (working paper, ILO).

10. Chaudhuri-Zohir, "Household Dynamics and Growth of Garment Industry in Bangladesh."

11. Kabeer and Mahmud, *Journal of International Development* 16 (1): 93–109.

12. World Bank, *How to Reform*, 18.

13. FIAS, *Special Economic Zones: Performance, Lessons Learned, and Implications for Zone Development*.

14. ODI (Overseas Development Institute), "Untangling the Links Between Trade, Poverty and Gender," 3; and Radhika Balakrishnan, *The Hidden Assembly Line: Gender Dynamics in Subcontracted Work in a Global Economy* (United States of America: Kumarian Press, Inc., 2002), 40.

15. Klasen and Lammana, quoted in *Gender and Growth*, DFID Briefing Note No. 5, March 2007.

16. Esteve-Volart, quoted in *Gender and Growth,* DFID Briefing Note No. 5, March 2007.

17. Nira Ramachandran, "Women and Food Security in South Asia," 8.

18. International Labour Organization, India Gender Profile.

19. U.K. Office for National Statistics.

20. For a useful summary of maternity benefits and gender-specific working hour restrictions, see World Bank, "Labour market regulations for women: are they beneficial?"

21. But in practice labor law reform in each country was not accompanied by fundamental reform in framework legislation, such as family and civil codes, thus limiting its impact.

22. Ellis et al., *Gender and Economic Growth in Uganda: Unleashing the Power of Women*, 76.

23. Yana Van der Meulen Rodgers, "Protecting Women and Promoting Equality in the Labor Market: Theory and Evidence," (World Bank, 1999), 9.

7

24. Joseph E. Zveglich, Jr., and Yana Van der Meulen Rodgers, "The Impact of Protective Measures for Female Workers," *Journal of Labor Economics,* 21 (3): 533.

25. DFID (Department for International Development), *Gender and Growth,* DFID Growth Team Briefing Note No. 5 (DFID, 2007), 5.

26. Law & Development Partnership, www.lawdevelopment.com; The Commission for Mediation and Arbitration, Tanzania.

27. Michael M. Lokshin, Marito Garcia, and Elena Glinskaya, "Effect of Early Childhood Development Programs on Women's Labour Force Participation and Older Children's Schooling in Kenya" (World Bank, 2000), 2.

28. Ellis et al., *Gender and Economic Growth in Kenya,* 82.

7

Foreign Investment Policy and Promotion

This Module Should be Used in Conjunction with the Core Module

This module on investment policy and promotion relates to programs and interventions designed to establish effective legal, regulatory, and policy frameworks for foreign investment and to support countries' investment promotion efforts. For the purposes of this section, IPP is taken as comprising (i) the development of national foreign direct investment and investment promotion strategies; (ii) sector targeting and outward promotion; (iii) the reform of investment law and policy frameworks; (iv) investor facilitation; and (v) investor aftercare and policy advocacy.

This module (i) provides tools to analyze the different impacts that investment policy and promotion can have on women and men (step 1 – diagnostic); (ii) provides solutions to address the gender issues revealed in the diagnostic (step 2 – solution design); and (iii) suggests ways to incorporate gender into the implementation and monitoring and evaluation of investment policy and promotion programs (step 3).

Summary

MODULE 8

Why Gender Matters

Enhanced foreign direct investment tends to affect men and women differently. Foreign investment has been highly significant in creating job opportunities for women, particularly in labor intensive, largely export-orientated industries, such as textiles; in call centers; and in the tourism sector. In many developing countries FDI has enabled women to enter the formal labor market for the first time.

FDI can also have negative impacts. Extractive industries and logging, for example, may adversely affect local people. Women may be particularly vulnerable to this (box 8.1). For FDI to achieve its key aims of improved growth and poverty reduction, it is important that policy makers and planners develop investment strategies cognizant of these broader economic and social issues and develop policies to address them.

BOX 8.1   The Impact of Logging on Women

The **Solomon Islands** emerged from conflict and social unrest in 2003 almost bankrupt. Economic recovery has taken place largely through logging operations by foreign investors. About a third of the country's 10 percent growth in 2007 was due to logging. The industry employs about 5,000 people—mainly men. Although logging has been the most significant factor in the Solomon Islands' economic recovery, its impact has been controversial, and most commentators regard its impact on women to have been largely detrimental. This is the result of (i) loss of women's land rights even in areas where the land is held on a matrilineal basis and women should have been—but were not—involved in the decision to grant logging rights; (ii) the lack of jobs for women resulting from logging operations; (iii) the payment of royalties by logging companies to land holding groups that largely exclude women; and (iv) serious and credible allegations of sexual exploitation of young women and girls in rural areas by foreign loggers. Results have included social unrest and demonstrations (some of them violent) by women in logging areas and challenges in the courts by women who have lost their land rights.

Policy responses to these gender issues could have included

- legal protection for women's land rights in logging areas, including measures to ensure they are involved in decision-making processes;
- improved legal protections for women as well as men entitled to royalties from logging; and
- protection for vulnerable women and young girls in logging areas in relation to sexual exploitation.

Source: IFC 2009.

8

As noted previously, foreign investment can be extremely positive in creating significant job opportunities for women. And evidence is emerging that when more women work in the formal sector, it is better for the country as a whole. Employing greater numbers of women is associated with enhanced growth and productivity (see box). It also tends to improve social outcomes—putting money into the hands of women results in better health and education for households.

In 2003, between 0.9 percent and 1.7 percent of the regional growth difference between the **East Asia and the Pacific** and **Middle East and North Africa** regions can be accounted for by gender gaps in labor force participation and education.[1]

Research undertaken in **India** suggests that women's limited labor market participation can result in reduced labor productivity. Increasing the ratio of women employees increased output by as much as 50 percent. Increasing women's engagement in management also improved firm performance and innovation.[2]

But there is mounting evidence that as industries upgrade, women can lose jobs to men, in part because of skill differences but also as a result of social norms that type technical jobs as "male."[3] Whatever the cause, the result is that women can get pushed down the production chain into subcontracted work.[4] Households, communities, and economies thus lose out on the gains that can be achieved by enhanced female labor force participation. If these issues are anticipated and understood, policy responses are possible within the context of FDI and sector targeting strategies. These could include the following:

- skills training for women
- improved employment practices and policies enforced through labor laws
- enhanced social infrastructure such as child care and maternity leave.

FDI also offers women the opportunity of enhanced employment opportunities through participating in foreign investors' supply chains. Yet women can lose out on this opportunity, resulting in a loss of broader economic and social benefits. This is because female-headed enterprises tend to be much smaller than those headed by men, often having only one or two employees. In Ethiopia, Kenya, and Tanzania, for example, the vast majority of women's enterprises employ only the owner—and thus cannot even be classified in the small and medium enterprise category.[5] Even in the most developed countries, female-owned enterprises are underrepresented among technology and export-oriented firms. Large foreign investors typically prefer to source from similarly large supply firms in order to hold down transaction costs. And women's more limited access to capital makes it difficult for them to respond quickly to changing markets, a frequent requirement for doing business with multinational companies. Other constraining factors are lack of access to business

8

training, networks, and opportunities to gain management experience. Again, policies can be developed within the context of an investment strategy to address these issues.

One obvious policy response is to ensure that female-headed businesses are able to benefit from the services offered by investment promotion agencies in relation to supplier development. Gender biases my not be obvious, but international evidence shows that women can be at a disadvantage when they interact with public/quasi-public authorities (see box). There can be a climate of discriminatory treatment that discourages women from dealing with public authorities by making it too time consuming and uncertain. It is important to ensure that investment promotion and aftercare facilities are as effective in the service they provide to both female and male clients.

Research into public administration in **India** found that women had to wait on average 37 percent longer than men to see the same local government official. Women of approximately the same income as men were three times more likely to be queue-jumped, and 16 percent of women reported sexual harassment from local government officials.[6]

A survey in **Bangladesh** found that government officials were more likely to target female applicants for informal "speed payments" as they were assumed to have a male provider.[7]

Step 1   Diagnostics

Step 1 provides tools to analyze

(i) the different impacts that strategies, policies, and laws to encourage foreign investment can have on women and men. This analysis will enable investment strategies and policies to be developed that (a) to the greatest extent possible provide benefits to women as well as men and (b) address any negative impacts on women that enhanced FDI may have.

(ii) the extent to which investment facilitation and aftercare initiatives benefit female as well as male investors. This analysis will enable investment promotion agencies to provide effective services to their female as well as their male clients.

(iii) the degree to which female as well as male investors are engaged in investment policy development and advocacy. If women's interests are effectively represented in investment policy development, such policies are more likely to benefit women as well as men, and potential negative impacts on women are more likely to be addressed.

> The critical steps to be taken during an initial project design phase (in the absence of a full diagnostic at that point) are identified by a magnifying glass icon. 🔍

1.1   Consider Impact of Enhanced FDI on Women

🔍 For the reasons explained in the "Why Gender Matters" section, policies and strategies to encourage FDI need to be developed taking into account the different impacts that enhanced FDI may have on women and men. Key issues to consider are as follows:

- The sectors targeted for FDI. The sectors in which a country is competitive need to be identified and targeted for enhanced investment. Then, to develop policies to maximize the growth and poverty reduction impacts of such sector targeting, consider
  - the extent to which women are represented in targeted sectors—as employees or as business owners;
  - the possibility of opportunities for women to participate in supply chains (as employees or as entrepreneurs).
- The extent to which women are likely to benefit from the enhanced employment and business opportunities that enhanced FDI may bring will be based on the following:
  - Are there differences in the education and training levels and participation rates of women and men?

8

- Do labor laws outlaw discrimination on the basis of gender, marital status, and pregnancy?
- Do women have access to the same information networks—both about employment opportunities and about opportunities to enter supply chains created by FDI?

> Evidence suggests that young women may have less access to broad social networks to aid in their job search and, consequently, have less information with which to make good decisions on sector and occupation.[8]

1.2 Review Legal and Regulatory Framework for Investment

If the country has an investment code, it should be reviewed to ensure that it is equally facilitative for both female and male investors. Overarching investment codes can apply to both foreign and local investors. The code itself is unlikely to contain provisions that discriminate against women, but consideration should be given to the extent to which the code overrides any discriminatory provisions in the country's legal framework. Key areas to consider are

- the overarching legal framework relating to the position of women—in particular in the constitution, family law, inheritance law, and property law (see core module);
- business entry and operations (see module 2);
- tax policy and administration (see module 3); and
- secured lending (see module 5).

Local lawyers with insights into gender issues should, if possible, be consulted for assistance with undertaking this review, for example, women's lawyers associations and nongovernmental organizations providing legal advice to women.

1.3 Undertake Institutional Gender Equality Assessment on Investment Promotion Authority

The investment-promotion authority administering the investment policy and promotion (IPP) program (marketing the country as an investment destination, facilitating investment, and providing investor aftercare) should be reviewed to ensure it has incorporated gender in its operations. Annex A contains a checklist of key issues to include.

Where the investment promotion authority has been in existence for some time, it may be helpful to undertake a gender-disaggregated client satisfaction survey to address some of the issues in annex A.

8

1.4 Consider the Extent to Which Women's Interests Are Represented in Investment Policy Development

The issues discussed in the diagnostics section of module 1 (Public-Private Dialogue) should be carefully considered in relation to the development of a country's investment strategy and policies.

8

Step 2   Solution Design

The diagnostic will reveal the extent to which a country's investment policies and promotion initiatives provide equal benefit to women as well as men. Step 2 sets out possible approaches to address issues revealed. Step 2.1 is the starting point for solution design—an agreement by key stakeholders about what the IPP program is intended to achieve in relation to men and women.

2.1   Agree on Gender-Related Program Results

The specific results that the IPP program is seeking in relation to gender should be identified up front, on the basis of the key issues highlighted in the diagnostic phase. Specific gender-disaggregated indicators should be agreed upon by key stakeholders. Possible indicators may include the number of men and women in the formal labor market.

2.2   Develop Interventions to Help Women to Benefit from Enhanced Investment

As discussed in the "Why Gender Matters" section of this module, enhanced female participation in the formal labor market tends to be associated with improved economic and social outcomes. Despite this, women frequently are not as well placed as their male counterparts to access the nontraditional and more highly paid employment and business opportunities that enhanced investment may bring. Women can be disadvantaged by poorer access to secondary schooling, early marriage and childbearing, and their "double time burden."[9] These broad social issues lie outside the scope of most IPP programs. But when developing an investment strategy, it will be useful to consider measures that could make it more possible for women to benefit from enhanced levels of investment, both as employees and as investors. Possible solutions include the following:

- Enhance information on employment and business opportunities open to women as a result of enhanced investment, for example, through targeted job counseling services or interactions with women's business and employee associations.
- Enhance women's opportunities to access training programs, for example, through child care provision (see box).

Evidence from demand-driven training programs in **Latin America** is that child care subsidies are an important tool for increasing young women's participation in training programs.[10]

8

- Enact labor laws prohibiting gender-based discrimination (see module 7 – Special Economic Zones).
- Encourage provision of affordable child care services for employees.

2.3 Undertake "Female-Friendly" Investment Promotion

A country's marketing or branding strategy could stress its "female-friendly" credentials as an investment destination. A country may also wish to focus on its potential for ethical investment and corporate social responsibility initiatives, including fair treatment for female employees (see examples from Poland and Cambodia in box).

Poland's Trade and Investment Promotion authority organized a *Successful Women 2008* trade show in Hungary, showcasing female-led enterprises.

In **Cambodia** the *Better Factories Cambodia* initiative promoted improved labor standards, including for women.

2.4 Ensure Investment Laws Are Gender Neutral

If the diagnostic has revealed specific laws that discriminate against female investors, action should be taken to reform or repeal them. It may well be that such laws contravene gender equality provisions in the country's constitution or international treaty obligations.

2.5 Ensure Women Can Benefit Equally from Investor Facilitation and Aftercare Services

Measures should be taken to address the issues raised in the gender equality checklist in annex A to ensure that investment promotion authorities provide services and operate in a manner that is equally relevant to female and to male clients.

2.6 Ensure Women's Voices Are Properly Represented in Investment Policy Development

The issues discussed in the solution design section of module 1 (Public-Private Dialogue) should be addressed in relation to the development of a country's investment strategy and policies.

8

Step 3 Implementation and M&E

The general points on implementation and monitoring and evaluation in the core module should be applied to IPP programs. In addition, the following issues should be considered in relation to M&E.

3.1 Put in Place Systems to Gather Gender-Disaggregated Data within the IPP Program

The IPP program's M&E system should be designed to gather basic gender-disaggregated data to enable the impact of the program on women, both as employees and as investors, to be assessed. Depending on the agreed-on program impacts, this could include

- the number of men and women in formal labor market;
- the number of men and women in skilled jobs and supervisory positions in the formal labor market; and
- a change in male and female wage levels.

3.2 Incorporate Indicators that Highlight Gender Aspects of the Program

Gender should also be incorporated in output and outcome level IPP program indicators. Examples are provided in table 8.1.

Table 8.1: M&E Indicators

Indicator/Data required	Gender focus (Gender disaggregation)	Source of data
Output indicators		
• Number of operational manuals produced • Training and outreach	• Qualitative indicator: gender-inclusive focus; gender issues articulated and addressed • Core indicator: number and/or percentage men and women participating or benefiting	• Manuals produced • Agency management • Focus group discussions (FGDs) • Interviews with businesswomen
• Number of surveys • Economic assessments produced	• Inclusion of gender-disaggregated data	• Survey reports • Investment Promotion Authority management

8

(Continued)

Table 8.1: M&E Indicators (*Continued*)

Indicator/Data required	Gender focus (Gender disaggregation)	Source of data
• Investment policies promoted	• Qualitative assessment: extent to which they address gender issues • Responsiveness to women investors	• Policy statements • FGDs • Women investors Business associations
Outcome indicators		
• Investment inquiries (leading to new investment) in targeted sectors	• Disaggregate by gender of investor	• Agency records • Tracking surveys
• User perceptions of services provided by the promotion agency	• Disaggregate by gender	• FGDs • Women investors • Business associations • Agency records
• Improved investment promotion agency operation and accessibility	• Welcoming of women • Percentage of men and women managers and staff in the agency	• FGDs • Agency management

8

Annex A   Institutional Gender Equality Checklist

1. Does the investment promotion authority have gender-disaggregated data, for example, on ownership of firms with investment licenses, inquiries, employment created by FDI?

2. Does the investment promotion authority have formal links with women's organizations (business associations, women's employees associations) for consultation and input into policy development, management, operations, and advocacy?

3. Are women or women's business organizations included in the investment promotion authority's governance structures, for example, advisory council, management board, or board of directors?

4. Does the investment promotion authority's customer charter, operational manual, and so on, include reference to gender equality issues?

5. Are women employed in the investment promotion authority, especially at levels where they interact with the public and at decision-making levels?

6. Are staff trained to handle gender issues sensitively?

7. Is the physical environment of the investment promotion authority one in which women would feel comfortable?

8. Are institutional systems in place to monitor gender-disaggregated results, and are these regularly reported on?

9. Is gender equality seen as an explicit goal of the organization?

10. Are gender equality perspectives evident in the institution's major policy and planning documents guiding the work of the institution?

8

Notes

1. S. Klasen and F. Lammana, *The Impact of Gender Inequality in Education and Employment on Economic Growth in the Middle East and North Africa* (World Bank, 2003).

2. B. Esteve-Volart, "Gender Discrimination and Growth: Theory and Evidence from India" (STICERD, 2004).

3. Gunseli Berik, Yana van der Meulen Rodgers, and Joseph E. Zveglich, Jr. *International Trade and Wage Discrimination: Evidence from East Asia* (World Bank, 2003); Elizabeth Fussell, "Making labour flexible: The recomposition of Tijuana's *maquiladora* female labour force," *Feminist Economics* 6 (3): 59–79.

4. E. Braunstein, *Foreign Direct Investment, Development and Gender Equity: A Review of Research and Policy* (United Nations Research Institute for Social Development, March 2006). See also Practitioners' Guide section on special economic zones.

5. International Labour Organization, "Supporting Growth-Oriented Women Entrepreneurs in Ethiopia, Kenya, and Tanzania."

6. S. Corbridge, "Gender, Corruption and the State: Tales from Eastern India," 2007.

7. Government of Bangladesh. *Governance, Management and Performance in Health and Education Facilities in Bangladesh: 2007* (Oxford Policy Management, Financial Management Reform Program, Ministry of Finance).

8. Ruth Levine, "Girls Count: A Global Investment and Action Agenda" (Center for Global Development, 2008); A. Malhotra and D. De Graff, "Entry versus Success in the Labour Force: Young Women's Employment in Sri Lanka," *World Development* 25 (3): 379–94; and World Bank, "The Economic Participation of Adolescent Girls and Young Women: Why Does It Matter?" PREM Notes Gender, No. 128.

9. The need to combine employment with domestic responsibilities. See Core Module for discussion.

10. H. Ñopo. et al., "Occupational Training to Reduce Gender Segregation: The Impacts of ProJoven" (World Bank, 2007); and World Bank, "The Economic Participation of Adolescent Girls and Young Women: Why Does It Matter?" PREM Notes Gender, No. 128.

8

Bibliography

About.com: Women in Business. http://womeninbusiness.about.com/od/billsandlaws/a/hr5050-wbo-act.htm (Accessed on September 2, 2009).

ADB (Asian Development Bank). 2006. "Gender, Law, and Policy in ADB Operations: A Tool Kit," ADB, Philippines.

Africa Union. 2003. Protocol to the African Charter on Human and Peoples' Rights on the Rights of Women in Africa. http://www.africa-union.org/root/au/Documents/Treaties/Text/Protocol%20on%20the%20Rights%20of%20Women.pdf.

Baliamoune-Lutz, Mina. 2007. "Globalisation and Gender Inequality: Is Africa Different?" *Journal of African Economies* 16 (2): 301–348.

Bangladesh Export Processing Zone Authority (BEPZA). 2008. "Export Processing Zones (EPZs) in Bangladesh: An Attractive Investment Destination."

Barnett, K., and Grown, C. 2004. *Gender Impacts of Government Revenue Collection: The Case of Taxation.* London: Commonwealth Secretariat. www.undp.org/women/CD-Gender-and-Budgets-2004/3.3-revenues.htm#1.

Bhattacharya, Debapriya. 1998. Export Processing Zones in Bangladesh: Economic Impact and Social Issues. Working Paper No. 80, International Labour Organization, Geneva.

Bhorat, H. 2000. "Are wage adjustments an effective mechanism for poverty alleviation? Some simulations for domestic and farm workers," TPS Annual Conference, Johannesburg, September 18–20. Quoted in DFID Briefing Note No. 5, *Gender and Growth,* March 2007.

Berik, Gunseli and Yana van der Rodgers. 2008. "Options for Enforcing Labour Standards: Lessons from Bangladesh and Cambodia." *Journal of International Development.* 18 (8): 1081–1104. Published online in Wiley InterScience. www.interscience.wiley.com DOI: 10.1002/jid.1534.

Berik, Gunseli, Yana van der Meulen Rodgers, and Joseph E. Zveglich, Jr. 2003. *International Trade and Wage Discrimination: Evidence from East Asia.* World Bank Policy Research Working Paper No. 3111, World Bank, Washington, DC.

Besley, T., R. Burgess, and B. Esteve-Volart. 2004. "Operationalising Pro-Poor Growth: India Case Study." Working paper. DFID, London.

Blackden, C. M., Canagarajah S., Klasen S., Lawson D. 2005 (Nov). "Gender and Growth in Sub-Saharan Africa: Issues and Evidence," Institute for Development Policy and Management, Manchester.

Blackden, C. M., and Quentin Wodon, eds. 2006. "Gender, Time Use, and Poverty in Sub-Saharan Africa," World Bank Working Paper No. 73, Washington, DC.

Blumberg, Rae Lesser. 1988. "Income Under Female vs. Male Control: Hypotheses from a Theory and Data from the Third World." *Journal of Family Issues* 9 (1): 51–84.

Boschini, A. 2003. "The Impact of Gender Stereotypes on Economic Growth." Working Paper. Department of Economics, University of Stockholm.

Braunstein, E. March 2006. "Foreign Direct Investment, Development and Gender Equity: A Review of Research and Policy." Occasional Paper Gender Policy 12. United Nations Research Institute for Social Development. Geneva.

Budlender, Debbie. 2004. *Why should we care about unpaid work.* UNIFEM, New York.

Busse, M. and P. Nunnenkamp. 2009. "Gender Disparity in Education and the International Competition for Foreign Direct Investment" *Feminist Economics* 15 (3): 61–90.

Catalyst. 2004. "The Bottom Line: Connecting Corporate Performance and Gender Diversity." http://www.catalyst.org/file/44/the%20bottom%20line%20connecting%20corporate%20performance%20and%20gender%20diversity.pdf.

The Coalition of Women Business Associations (CAFA). http://www.cafa.ro/project1_en_about.html (accessed October 19, 2009).

Cavalcanti, T. and J. Tavares. 2007. "The Output Cost of Gender Discrimination: A Model-Based Macroeconomic Estimate." Working paper. Universidade Nova de Lisboa and Center for Economic Policy Research, Lisbon.

CEDAW (Convention on the Elimination of Discrimination Against Women). http://unifem-eseasia.org/projects/Cedaw/shadowreports.html.

CEDAW (Combined Initial, Second, and Third Reports on the Convention on the Elimination of All Forms of Discrimination Against Women). September 2004. CEDAW/C/VUT/1-3.

CEDAW (Convention on the Elimination of Discrimination Against Women). http://www.un.org/womenwatch/daw/cedaw/NGO_Information_note_CEDAW.pdf.

Center for International Private Enterprise (CIPE) strengthens democracy around the globe through private enterprise and market-oriented reform. CIPE is one of the four core institutes of the National Endowment for Democracy and a nonprofit affiliate of the U.S. Chamber of Commerce.

Center of Arab Women for Training and Research, and IFC GEM. June 2007. *Women Entrepreneurs* in the Middle East and North Africa: Characteristics, Contributions and Challenges. Surveys conducted in Bahrain, Jordan, Lebanon, Tunisia, and the United Arab Emirates in 2006.

Chamlou, Nadereh. 2008. *The Environment for Women's Entrepreneurship in the Middle East and North Africa Region.* World Bank, Washington DC.

Chaudhuri-Zohir, Salma. 2000. "Household Dynamics and Growth of Garment Industry in Bangladesh." Proceedings of a National Seminar on the Growth of the Garment Industry in Bangladesh: Economic and Social Dimensions. BIDS and Oxfam Bangladesh, Dhaka.

Corbridge, S. 2007. "Gender, Corruption and the State: Tales from Eastern India," in DFID (Department for International Development). 2008 (July). *The Gender Manual. A Practical Guide.* London.

Cueva's 2006 index, based on the Cinganelli-Richards scores on government commitment and capacity to enforce women's social, economic and cultural rights with the addition of variables on international rights instruments.

Cutura, J. 2006. "Lessons of Experience in Technical Assistance Making the Investment Climate Work for Women—Moving a Report from a Bookshelf into Action," IFC GEM, Washington, DC.

DAI Europe & WISE Development. 2007 (Dec.). Monitoring and Evaluation for Business Environment Reform: A Toolkit for Practitioners. Final draft for IFC SME Advisory Services. Washington, DC, June 2008.

Dejene, Y. 2001. "Women's Cross-Border Trade in West Africa," *WIDTECH Information Bulletin.*

Desai, Sonalde and Kiersten Johnson. 2005. "Women's Decisionmaking and Child Health," in Sunitor Kishor, ed., *A Focus on Gender: Collected papers on gender using DHS data.* Calverton, MD: ORC Macro and U.S. Agency for International Development.

DFID (U.K. Department for International Development). 2000 (Sept). "Poverty Elimination and the Empowerment of Women," London.

———. March 2007. Briefing Note No. 5, *Gender and Growth.*

———. April 2007. "Gender Equality (Duty) Scheme 2007–2010," DFID, London.

DFID (U.K. Department for International Development). July 2008. *The Gender Manual: A Practical Guide.* DFID, London.

Dowuona-Hammond, C. 2007. *Enterprise Development—African and Global Lessons for More Effective Donor Practices from Women's Perspective: Improved Land And Property Rights.* Deutsche Gesellschaft für Technische Zusammenarbeit (GTZ) GmbH Programme Promoting Gender Equality and Women's Rights, Eschborn, 2008.

Eissa, Nada. 1995. "Taxation and Labour Supply of Married Women: The Tax Reform Act of 1986 as a Natural Experiment." NBER Working Paper No. w5023, Cambridge, MA: National Bureau for Economic Research.

Ellis, A., Cutura J., Dione N., Gillson I., Manuel C., Thongori J. 2007. *Gender and Economic Growth in Kenya—Unleashing the Power of Women.* Washington, DC: World Bank.

Ellis, A., Manuel C., and Blackden M. 2006. *Gender and Economic Growth in Uganda— Unleashing the Power of Women.* Washington, DC: World Bank.

Ellis, A., et al. 2007. Tanzania Gender and Growth Assessment: *Gender and Economic Growth in Tanzania: Creating Opportunities for Women.* Washington, DC: World Bank.

Ellis, A., et al. 2008. *Doing Business: Women in Africa.* Washington, DC: World Bank.

Esim, Simel. 2000. "Impact of Government Budgets on Poverty and Gender Equality." International Center for Research on Women (ICRW). Paper prepared for the Inter-Agency Workshop on Improving the Effectiveness of Integrating Gender Into Government Budgets: Commonwealth Secretariat, Marlborough House, London, April 26–27, 2000.

Esteve-Volart. 2004. "Gender Discrimination and Growth: Theory and Evidence from India." Development Economics Discussion Paper no 42. Suntory and Toyota International

Centres for Economics and Related Disciplines. London School of Economics and Political Science. London.

FAO (Food and Agriculture Organization). 1998. Rural Women and Food Security: Current Situation and Perspectives. Rome.

FIAS (Foreign Investment Advisory Service). Business Taxation. Financial and Private Sector Development. IFC, Washington, DC. http://www.fias.net/ifcext/fias.nsf/Content/Pubs _BusinessTaxation?OpenDocument&StartPagePublicationsbyProductLinesBusiness Taxation=2 (Accessed on September 2, 2009).

FIAS (Foreign Investment Advisory Service). 2007. "BEE Business Line Regional Strategy-Africa Region, FY07–10," FIAS Africa Office.

FIAS. April 2008. "Special Economic Zones: Performance, Lessons Learned, and Implications for Zone Development," FIAS, Washington, DC.

FIAS. 2008. "Trade Logistics Advisory Programme: Easing Access to Markets," FIAS Washington, DC.

FIAS. May 2008. *Trade Logistics Advisory Program: Building Competitive Trade Logistics for Global Markets.* Powerpoint presentation to FIAS conference, Washington, DC, May, 2009.

FIAS. March 2006. *A Manual for the Identification and Removal of Administrative Barriers to Investment,* FIAS, Washington, DC.

FinScope. 2005. http://www.finscope.co.za/about.html (Accessed August 2, 2009).

Fussell, Elizabeth. 2000. "Making Labour Flexible: The Recomposition of Tijuana's *Maquiladora* Female Labour Force." *Feminist Economics* 6 (3): 59–79.

Gamser, M., Kadritzke, R., Waddington, R. 2005. "Reforming the Business Enabling Environment: Mechanisms and Processes for Private-Public Sector Dialogue." This paper is based on work undertaken for DFID by Bannock Consulting Ltd.

GlobalRights.org—*Partners for Justice Online.* 2006. http://www.globalrights.org/site/Message Viewer?em_id=5101.0 (Accessed August 3, 2009).

Global Banking Alliance for Women. http://www.gbaforwomen.org/.

Government of Rwanda. 2006. *Organic Law No 31/2006 of 14/08/2006 on Organisation, Jurisdiction, Competence and Functioning of the Mediation Committee* Article 4.

Gindling, Timothy, and Maria Crummett. 1997. "Maternity Leave Legislation and the Work and Pay of Women in Costa Rica." Working paper. University of Maryland Baltimore County, Maryland. Quoted in Yana van der Meulen Rodgers. 1999 (Nov). *Protecting Women and Promoting Equality in the Labor Market: Theory and Evidence.* Policy Research Report on Gender and Development Working Paper Series, No. 6. Washington, DC: World Bank.

Giovarelli, R. 2007 (May). *Legal Aspects of Women and Land and Property Rights.*

Global Knowledge Partnership. 2007. *Handbook on Women Owned SMEs: Challenges and Opportunities in Policies and Programmes.* International Organisation for Knowledge Economy and Enterprise Development (IKED), Malmo, Sweden.

Government of Bangladesh. 2007. G*overnance, Management and Performance in Health and Education Facilities in Bangladesh.* Oxford Policy Management, Financial Management Reform Program, Ministry of Finance.

Government of Germany. 2007. *Working Aid: Gender Impact Assessment: Gender Mainstreaming in the Preparation of Legislation.* Federal Ministry for Family Affairs, Senior Citizens, Women and Youth. Germany.

Government of the United States. U.S.Women's Business Ownership Act of 1988 and Executive Order 12138.About.com: Women in Business. http://womeninbusiness.about.com/od/billsandlaws/a/hr5050-wbo-act.htm (Accessed on October 14, 2009).

Haddad, Lawrence, John Hoddinott, and Harold Alderman. 1997. *Intrahousehold Resource Allocation in Developing Countries: Models, Methods, and Policy.* Baltimore, MD: Johns Hopkins University Press.

Herzberg. 2008. *PPD Product Review.* Powerpoint Presentation, IFC. November 2008.

Herzberg, Benjamin. 2009. *Basics of Monitoring and Evaluation—M&E for Public-Private Dialogue*, Presentation made at the 2009 PPD Workshop, Vienna, Austria, April. Accessed October 2009 at the PPD Website: http://www.publicprivatedialogue.org/workshop%202009/

ICRW (International Center for Research on Women). 2000 (Apr). "Impact of Government Budgets on Poverty and Gender Equality." Paper prepared for the Inter-Agency Workshop on Improving the Effectiveness of Integrating Gender Into Government Budgets: Commonwealth Secretariat. Marlborough House, London, 26–27.

IFC GEM in Bahrain, Jordan, Lebanon, Tunisia and the United Arab Emirates in 2006. *Women Entrepreneurs in the Middle East and North Africa: Characteristics, Contributions and Challenges* (June 2007). The Center of Arab Women for Training and Research and IFC GEM.

IFC (International Finance Corporation). 2008. M&E Handbook.

IFC (International Finance Corporation). Trade Logistics team Rwanda process mapping 2008.

IFC (International Finance Corporation). Unpublished. *Rwanda: Review of the Legal and Regulatory Framework for Business from a Legal Perspective.* IFC, Washington, DC.

IFC 2005, Access to Finance for Women Entrepreneurs in South Africa: Challenges and Opportunities.

IFC. 2007. "Voices of Vietnamese Women Entrepreneurs," IFC GEM, Washington, DC.

IFC. 2008. *Rwanda: Voices of Women Entrepreneurs.* IFC, Washington, DC.

IFC GEM (International Finance Corporation Gender Entrepreneurship Markets). 2006. *Voices of Women Entrepreneurs in Kenya.* IFC GEM, Washington, DC.

———. 2006 (Nov). "Women Entrepreneurs and Access to Finance: Program Profiles from Around the World." IFC GEM, Washington, DC.

———. 2007. "Gender and Economic Growth Assessment for Ghana 2007," IFC GEM, Washington, DC.

———. 2007. "Voices of Women Entrepreneurs in Tanzania," IFC GEM, Washington, DC.

IFC SME (International Finance Corporation Small and Medium Enterprise) Advisory Services. Dates various. Series of "Smart Lessons" reports. Washington, DC: IFC.

———. Dates various. Series of Toolkits and Handbooks for Monitoring and Evaluation of Various Aspects of Business Environment Programs (for example, licensing, taxation, business registration, ICT, ADR, import-export regulations, HIV-AIDS, and so on). Washington, DC: IFC.

IFC World Bank. (2009). *Business Taxation.* Retrieved August 3, 2009, from the IFC Financial & Private Sector Development Website:

ILO (International Labour Organization). ———. 1998. *Labour and Social Issues relating to Export Processing Zones*, Geneva.

———. 2008. Global Employment Trends for Women 2008. Geneva.

ILO (International Labour Organization). India Gender Profile.

ILO (International Labour Organization). 2004 (July). "Supporting Growth-Oriented Women Entrepreneurs in Ethiopia, Kenya and Tanzania."Overview report prepared by ILO SEED Programme and African Development Bank Private Sector Department.

International Poverty Centre. 2008 (Jan). Poverty in Focus—Special edition of 12 articles on gender and poverty, IPC, Brasilia, Brazil.

IWRAW Asia Pacific (International Women's Rights Action Watch). 2007 (Jan). Vanuatu NGO Shadow Report on the Implementation of the Convention on the Elimination of All Forms of Discrimination Against Women. www.iwraw-ap.org/resources/pdf/Vanuatu .pdf.

Kabeer, Naila, and Simeen Mahmud. 2004. "*Globalization, Gender and Poverty: Bangladeshi Women Workers in Export and Local Markets.*" *Journal of International Development* 16 (1): 93–109.

———. 2004. "*Rags, Riches and Women Workers: Export Oriented Garment Manufacturing in Bangladesh.*" *In Marilyn Carr (ed.), Chains of Fortune: Linking Women Producers and Workers with Global Markets, 134–62.* London: Commonwealth Secretariat.

Kaufman, Daniel, and Shang Jin-Wei. 2000 (Mar). "Does Grease Money Speed up the Wheels of Commerce?" World Bank, Washington, DC.

Kikeri, S., et al. 2006. "Reforming the Investment Climate: Lessons for Practitioners," IFC, Washington, DC.

Klasen, S., and F. Lammana. 2003. *The Impact of Gender Inequality in Education and Employment Economic Growth in the Middle East and North Africa* (Background paper for the World Bank Study: Women in the Public Sphere (Washington, DC: The World Bank). Quoted in DFID Briefing Note No. 5, *Gender and Growth,* March 2007.

Klasen, S. and F. Lamanna. "The Impact Gender Inequality in Education and Employment on Economic Growth in Developing Countries," *Feminist Economics.* (2009) 15 (3): 91–132.

Knowles, Stephen, Paula Lorgelly, and P. Dorian Owen. 2002. "Are Educational Gender Gaps a Brake on Economic Development? Some Cross-Country Empirical Evidence." *Oxford Economic Papers* 54 (1): 118–49.

Law & Development Partnership, The. 2007. "The Legal Dimensions of Women's Economic Empowerment: A World Bank Consultations-Discussion Paper on Access to Credit and Finance: Beyond Microfinance," World Bank, Washington, DC.

Levine, Ruth et al. 2008. "Girls Count: A Global Investment and Action Agenda," Center for Global Development, Washington, DC.

Lokshin, Glinskaya, and M. E. Garcia. 2000. "Effect of Early Childhood Development Programs on Women's Labour Force Participation and Older Children's Schooling in Kenya." Background paper for "*Engendering Development*," World Bank, Washington. http://www.worldbank.org/gender/prr/wp15.pdf.

Macculloch F. 2007. "Gender and Economic Growth in Tanzania—Unleashing the Power of Women." IFC GEM, Washington, DC.

Malhotra, A. and De Graff, D. 1997. *Entry Versus Success in the Labour Force: Young Women's Employment in Sri Lanka* World Development 25 (3): 379–94, quoted in Morrison, A. and S. Sabarwal, "The Economic Participation of Adolescent Girls and Young Women: Why Does It Matter?" PREM Notes Gender, No. 128, December 2008.

Malhotra, M., et al. 2007. *Expanding Access to Finance: Good Practices and Policies for Micro, Small, and Medium Enterprises*, World Bank Institute Learning Resource Series. Washington, DC: World Bank.

Mason, A. and Elizabeth King. "Engendering Development Gender Equality in Rights, Resources, and Voice," Policy Research Report 21776, World Bank, Washington, DC.

Mazumdar, I. 2006. *Impact of Globalization on Women Workers in Garment Exports—the Indian Experience: in Trade, Globalisation and Gender Evidence from South Asia*, 2006 ed Veena Jha, UNIFEM South Asia Regional Office, 2006, in DFID Briefing Note No. 5, *Gender and Growth*, March 2007.

McDowell, L. 2008. "Gender, Employment and Identity," *St John's College Magazine*, Oxford, Autumn.

MIGA (Multilateral Investment Guarantee Agency). 2001. Investment Promotion Toolkit, World Bank, Washington, DC.

Morrison, Andrew, et al. Sept 2007. "Gender Equality, Poverty and Economic Growth," Gender & Development Group, World Bank, Washington, DC.

Morrison, Andrew, and Shwetlena Sabarwal. 2008. "The Economic Participation of Adolescent Girls and Young Women: Why Does It Matter?" PREM Notes Gender, No. 128, World Bank, Washington, DC.

Nabli, Mustapha, and Nadereh Chamlou. 2004. *Gender and Development in the Middle East and North Africa: Women in the Public Sphere*, MENA Development Report, World Bank, Washington, DC.

National Women's Business Council. U.S. Small Business Administration, Washington, D.C. http://www.nwbc.gov/.

Ñopo, H., Robles, M., and Saavedra J., et al. 2007. "Occupational Training to Reduce Gender Segregation: The Impacts of ProJoven," Research Development Working Paper No 623, World Bank, Washington, DC, quoted in Morrison, A. and S. Sabarwal, "The Economic Participation of Adolescent Girls and Young Women: Why Does It Matter?" PREM Notes Gender, No. 128, December 2008.

Nuchhi, Currier, and Cornelia Rotaru. 2009. "Women's Business Associations. Experiences from Around the World: South Asia." *Center for International Private Enterprise*. Center for International Private Enterprise, Washington D.C.

ODI (Overseas Development Institute). 2008 (Mar). *Untangling the Links Between Trade, Poverty and Gender,* Briefing Paper 28, ODI, London.

———. 2008 (Mar). *Untangling links between trade, poverty and gender.* Briefing Paper 38, ODI, London, and *Balakrishnan, R.* (ed.). 2002. *The Hidden Assembly Line: Gender Dynamics in Subcontracted Work in a Global Economy.* Bloomfield, CT: Kumarian Press.

OWIT (Organization of Women in International Trade). http://www.owit.org/en/Home/Index.aspx (Accessed September 2, 2009).

Pal, M. S. 1997. "Women Entrepreneurs and the Need for Financial Sector Reform," *Economic Reform Today,* Number Two (1997): 26–30.

Peberdy, S. A. 2000. "Border Crossings: Small Entrepreneurs and Cross Border Trade Between South Africa and Mozambique," *Journal of Economic and Social Geography* 91(4): 361–378.

Pitt, Mark, and Shahidur Khandker, 1998. "The Impact of Group-Based Credit Programs on Poor Households in Bangladesh: Does the Gender of Participants Matter?" *Journal of Political Economy* 106: 958–96.

PREM (Poverty Reduction and Economic Management Network). 2007. PREM Knowledge and Learning Forum 2007. Powerpoint Presentations on Employment and Gender in the Shared Growth Agenda, Washington, DC. April 25.

PREM (Poverty Reduction and Economic Management Network). 2004. *Labor market regulations for women: are they beneficial?,* PREM Notes 94, World Bank, Washington, DC.

Prowess. (2001). www.prowess.org.uk/publications.htm (accessed August 3, 2009). www.publicprivatedialogue.org. (accessed September 3, 2009).

Quisumbing, A. 1996. Male-Female Differences in Agricultural Productivity: Methodological Issues and Empirical Evidence. *World Development* 24 (10): 1579–95.

Quisumbing, Agnes R. (ed.). 2003. *Household Decisions, Gender and Development: A* synthesis of recent research. Washington, DC: International Food Policy Research Institute.

Rama, Martin. 1996. *The Consequences of Doubling the Minimum Wage: The Case of Indonesia.* Policy Research Working Paper 1643, World Bank, Washington, DC.

Ramachandran, Nira. 2006 (Nov). "Women and Food Security in South Asia." Research Paper prepared for the UNU-WIDER (United Nations University World Institute for Development Economics Research). Helsinki.

Richardson, Pat, Rhona Howarth, and Gerry Finnegan. 2004. "The Challenges of Growing Small Businesses: Insights from Women Entrepreneurs in Africa." InFocus Programme on Boosting Employment through Small Enterprise Development, ILO, Geneva.

Robinson, Nelcia. 2001. "Small Island States Caught Between Elephants and Hippos." Paper prepared for a Women and Development workshop, Copenhagen, October 27.

Rodgers, Yana van der Meulen. 1991 (Nov). "*Protecting Women and Promoting Equality in the Labour Market: Theory and Evidence.*" Policy Research Working Paper Series no. 6, The World Bank Development Research Group Poverty Reduction and Economic Management Network, World Bank, Washington, DC.

Ruiz Abril, Maria Elena. 2008. "Girls Vulnerability Assessment." Background paper for the preparation of project to promote the economic empowerment of young women in Liberia. World Bank, Washington, DC.

Sada, I. N., Adamu, F. L., Ahmad, A. 2005. "Promoting Women's Rights Through Sharia in Northern Nigeria." DFID, Nigeria and British Council.

SADC (Southern African Develoment Community). 2007. http://aceproject.org/ero-en/misc/SADC%20Draft%20Protocol%20on%20Gender%20and%20Development19-7-07.pdf (Accessed September 3, 2009).

Seguino, Stephanie, and James Lovinsky. 2009. "The Impact of Religiosity on Gender Attitudes and Outcomes." UNRISD background paper, United Nations Research Institute for Social Development, Geneva.

Special Economic Zones Practitioner's Guide: With Application to Conflict-Affected Countries. 2009. IFC ICAS.

Stiftung, Friedrich Ebert, and Collaborative Centre for Gender and Development. 2006. "Women and Cross Border Trade in East Africa: Opportunities and Challenges for Small-Scale Women Traders," Nairobi, Kenya.

Stotsky, Janet G. 2006. "Gender and its Relevance to Macroeconomic Policy: A Survey," IMF Working Paper No. 06/233, International Monetary Fund, Washington, DC.

———. June 2007. "Budgeting with Women in Mind." Finance & Development, IMF Quarterly Magazine 44 (2): Accessible at http://www.imf.org/external/pubs/ft/fandd/2007/06/stotsky.htm (Accessed September 3, 2009).

———. 1997. "Gender bias in tax systems." *Tax Notes International,* June 9.

Texas, State of. 1994. Report of the Gender Bias Task Force, Supreme Court of Texas.

Times Newspaper, The. 2008. *Justice is seen to be done as Elephant Toilet puts paid to the inconvenient courtroom.* 3:29 (December 3).

Tran-Nguyen, A., and A. Beviglia Zampetti, eds. 2004. *Trade and Gender: Opportunities and Challenges for Developing Countries,"* UNCTAD, New York and Geneva.

Uganda Ministry of Finance. 2002. Planning and Economic Development, De-regulation Project. http://www.apesma.asn.au/women/maternity_leave_around_the_world.asp.

Uganda Ministry of Finance. 2004.

Uganda Participatory Poverty Assessment Process. 2002. "Second Participatory Poverty Assessment Report," Ministry of Finance, Planning, and Economic Development, Kampala, in World Bank. 2005. *Uganda: From Periphery to Center, A Strategic Country Gender Assessment*, Report No. 30136-UG, Washington, DC.

U.K. Office For National Statistics. http://www.statistics.gov.uk/cci/nugget.asp?id=167 (last accessed September 4, 2009).

UN (United Nations). www.un.org/womenwatch/asp/user/list.asp?ParentID=4001 and www.un.org/womenwatch/daw/Review/english/news.htm (Accessed September 3, 2009).

UN. http://daccessdds.un.org/doc/UNDOC/GEN/N05/487/60/PDF/N0548760.pdf?OpenElement (Accessed September 3, 2009).

UNDP (United Nations Development Programme) *Human Development Report.* 1995.

UNFPA (United Nations Population Fund). http://www.unfpa.org/about/index.htm (Accessed September 3, 2009). http://www.un.org/millenniumgoals/ (Accessed September 3, 2009).

United Republic of Tanzania. 1996. "Report of the Commission on Corruption" ("The Warioba Report") (Dar-es-Salaam:1996); and Government of Kenya. 2003. "Report of the Integrity and Anti-Corruption Committee of the Judiciary of Kenya" (the "Ringera Report").

UNIFEM (United Nations Development Fund for Women). March 2006. "Promoting Gender Equality in New Aid Modalities and Partnerships—Discussion Paper," UNIFEM, New York.

———. 2007. *Removing Gender Biases from Judicial Processes.* UNIFEM, New York, http://www.unifem.org/gender_issues/voices_from_the_field/story.php?StoryID=612.

———. July 2006. *Promoting Gender Equality in New Aid Modalities and Partnerships—Experiences from Africa (Burundi Consultation Outcome Report)*, UNIFEM, New York.

———. Sept. 2007. "Capacity Development for Promoting Gender Equality in the Aid Effectiveness Agenda: Lessons from Sub-regional Consultations in Africa," UNIFEM, New York.

———. 2008. "Who Answers to Women? Gender & Accountability." UNIFEM, New York.

———. 2008/2009. *Progress of the World's Women 2008/2009: Who Answers to Women?* UNIFEM, New York.

USAID (U.S. Agency for International Development) RWANDA. Report on the Role of Women's legal rights in the family and in Rwandan Society. Women's Legal Rights Initiative Conference 2006, March 16, 2006.

U.S. Census Bureau. http://www.census.gov/ (accessed October 19, 2009).

U.S. Survey of Business Owners and the Self-Employed. http://www.census.gov/econ/sbo/

U.S. Small Business Administration, Washington, DC. http://www.sba.gov/aboutsba/sbaprograms/onlinewbc/index.html

Van Staveren, Irene, and Akram-Lodhi, A. Haroon. 2003. *A Gender Analysis of the Impact of Indirect Taxes on Small and Medium Enterprises in Vietnam.* The Hague, The Netherlands: Institute of Social Studies. Draft paper presented at the IAFFE Conference, University of the West Indies, Barbados, June 27–29.

Van der Meulen Rodgers, Yana. 1999 (Nov). "Protecting Women and Promoting Equality in the Labour Market: Theory and Evidence." Policy Research Working Paper Series No. 6, The World Bank Development Research Group Poverty Reduction and Economic Management Network,World Bank,Washington, DC.

World Bank. Enterprise Analysis Unit, World Bank, Washington, DC. www.enterprisesurveys.org (Accessed September 3, 2009).

———. 2003. "The Kenya Strategic Country Gender Assessment." PREM and ESSD, Africa Region, World Bank, Nairobi.

World Bank. 2004. Kenya Investment Climate Survey. World Bank, Washington, DC.

Word Bank. 2004 (Dec). PREM Notes No. 34, *Labour Market Regulations for Women: Are They Beneficial?* World Bank, Washington, DC.

World Bank. 2005. World Development Report. World Bank, Washington, DC.

World Bank. 2006. *Doing Business in 2006: Creating Jobs.* World Bank, Washington, DC, and IFC, Secured Lending Program, Washington, DC.

World Bank. 2006 (Nov). Business Licensing Reform: A Toolkit for Development Practitioners. World Bank Group Small and Medium Enterprise Department, World Bank, Washington, DC.

———. Sept. 2006. "Gender Equality as Smart Economics—A World Bank Group Gender Action Plan (Fiscal years 2007–10)," World Bank, Washington, DC.

———. 2006. "The PPD Handbook: A Toolkit for Business Environment Reformers." World Bank, Washington, DC.

———. 2007. "Doing Business 2007: How to Reform," World Bank, Washington, DC.

———. 2007. "Doing Business 2008—Opportunities for Women." Power point presentation to accompany launch of Gender Action Plan. World Bank, Washington, DC.

———. 2007. "Gender: Working Towards Greater Equality" (International Development Association (IDA) at Work Note to accompany launch of Gender Action Plan), World Bank, Washington, DC.

———. 2007. *Global Monitoring Report 2007, Chapter 3: Promoting Gender Equality and Women's Empowerment*, World Bank, Washington, DC.

———. 2007. "IDA at Work—Gender: Working Towards Greater Equality." Background paper to World Bank Gender Action Plan, World Bank, Washington, DC.

———. 2007. Gender Action Plan, http://web.worldbank.org/WBSITE/EXTERNAL/TOPICS/ EXTGENDER/0,,contentMDK:21983335~pagePK:210058~piPK:210062~the SitePK:336868,00.html (Accessed September 4, 2009).

———. 2007. *Millennium Development Goals Global Monitoring Report.* Washington, DC, 110.

———. 2007. *Environment for Women's Entrepreneurship in the Middle East and North Africa Region.* Washington, DC: World Bank. http://web.worldbank.org/WBSITE/EXTERNAL/ COUNTRIES/MENAEXT/0,,contentMDK:21517656~pagePK:146736~piPK:146830~the SitePK:256299,00.html (Accessed September 4, 2009).

———. 2007. Legal Department Report 2007. "El Rol del Marco Legal en el Empoderamiento Economico de la Mujer: el Caso de Honduras."

———. 2007. *Strategic Communications for Business Environment Reforms: A Guide To* Stakeholder Engagement and Reform Promotion, Part II, Case Studies. SME Department, World Bank,Washington, DC.

———. Doing Business Women in Africa. 2008. "Gone Rural." World Bank, Washington, DC.

———. 2009. "Doing Business 2009," World Bank, Washington D.C.

World Economic Forum—World Bank, and African Development Bank, *2007 Africa Competitiveness Report, Gender Chapter.* World Economic Forum, Geneva. 69–85.

World Economic Forum. 2008. Gender Gap Index, *Global Gender Gap Report,* Geneva.

Zveglich, Jr., Joseph E. and Yana Van der Meulen Rodgers. 2003. "The Impact of Protective Measures for Female Workers." Journal of Labor Economics, vol. 21, no. 3: pg. 533.

Index